An Introduction to ENG

Bernard Hesketh
and
Ivor Yorke

Focal Press
An imprint of Butterworth-Heinemann Ltd
Linacre House, Jordan Hill, Oxford OX2 8DP

ℝ A member of the Reed Elsevier group

OXFORD   LONDON   BOSTON
MUNICH   NEW DELHI   SINGAPORE   SYDNEY
TOKYO   TORONTO   WELLINGTON

First published 1993

British Library Cataloguing in Publication Data
A catalogue record for this book is available from the British Library

ISBN 0 240 51317 7

Library of Congress Cataloguing in Publication Data
A catalogue record for this book is available from the Library of Congress

Phototypeset by Deltatype Ltd, Ellesmere Port, Cheshire
Printed and bound in Great Britain

Contents

About the Authors

Bernard Hesketh was the first cameraman in Britain to shoot ENG material for broadcast transmission. He started his career with Pathé News, one of the leading cinema newsreel companies, before becoming a founder staff member of BBC Television News in 1955. He was the first television cameraman to be accredited to Buckingham Palace, but spent many of his 30 years with the BBC covering wars, including those in Cyprus, Vietnam and the Middle East. Some of his most memorable pictures were taken during the Falklands conflict of 1982. He also contributed to BBC Newsnight, Panorama and documentaries. In 1989 he was responsible for the recruitment and training of camera crews for Visnews' new Sky News Service, and covered Select and Standing Committees of Parliament. Bernard Hesketh was awarded the MBE in 1986 for services to the television industry. Sadly, after completing his work on this book, Bernard Hesketh died in April 1993, shortly before publication. *An Introduction to Eng* stands as a memorial to the professionalism in which he believed so strongly.

Ivor Yorke was a journalist on local newspapers and in Fleet Street before joining BBC Television News as a sub-editor in 1964. He went on to become a reporter, producer and editor on a wide range of BBC news programmes. After six years as Head of Journalist Training, he left the BBC in 1992 to establish Broadcast Techniques, his own training consultancy. Ivor Yorke is vice-chairman of the National Council for the Training of Broadcast Journalists, and chaired the national industry working party establishing standards for broadcast journalism and factual writing. He is the author of two previous Focal Press books, *The Technique of Television News*, and *Basic TV Reporting*.

Acknowledgements

The authors would very much like to acknowledge the generous help and guidance we have received from many people during this project, especially from those kind enough to allow us to reproduce illustrations in which they hold the copyright.

Our gratitude therefore to David Goldsmith for his technical advice, and Ian Aizlewood, Managing Director, Continental Microwave; Inspector Mike Alderson, Sussex Police; Caroline Allport, Metropolitan Police; Allan Anderson; Robert Beveridge, Health & Safety Executive; Ken Carter, Office for Pictorial Broadcasting, US Defense Department; Graham Clark and John Wykes, Audio Engineering; Ron Collins, Managing Director, OpTex; Neil Everton; Martin Freeman and Pat Beckwith, BBC Central Stills; Debbie Gaiger, Camerapix, for the use of her photograph of Mohammed Amin; Martin Hayes, Manager, BBC Shipping Services; John Hurley, Ikegami; Nick Jennings, Foreign Editor, Sky News; Gavan Kelly, Mutterbox; Rob Kirk, Editor, Thames News; Suzanne Levy, BBC New York; Steve McGuinness and Paula Midwood, Advent Communications; Randall Miles, Arri Lights; John Mills, Director of Public Relations, St John Ambulance; Gareth Price, Tom Hadley, Shige Morikawa, Sony Broadcast Communications; Ian Raisbeck, Alan Mann Helicopters; Roy Saatchi, Head of Local Programmes, BBC North; James Swanson, Flying Pictures, for photographic assistance; Rick Thompson, Head of News & Current Affairs, BBC Midlands; Brian Walker and Nigel Gardiner, PAG Ltd; Peter Wilkinson, specialist helicopter cameraman, ITN; Paul Whiting, Sennheiser UK Ltd.

Finally, special thanks to our wives, without whom none of this would have been possible: Kathleen Hesketh for her writing, word-processing skills and patience; Fred (Cynthia) Yorke for being prepared to let the decorating wait . . . again.

Introduction

It is less than 20 years since those responsible for collecting the raw material for factual TV programmes stopped going into the field with technology borrowed from another medium.

The pioneering TV news crews of the fifties, often recruits hired from the buccaneering but anachronistic cinema newsreel companies, went into action with equipment which, effective though it was for its time, had two inherent drawbacks. First, until the exposed material was put through a chemical development process not even the best cameraman (they usually *were* men) could be certain the images they had captured were exactly what they had seen in the viewfinder; and secondly, the time spent in the processing bath represented a frustrating delay before the events they had filmed – no matter how dramatic or important they were – were ready to reach the screen.

Over the years the manufacturers of film stock worked hard to reduce the wait, but by the time they had brought it down to an insignificant few minutes per 100ft (30m), it was too late. For daily TV journalism, at least, the revolution was already over. Newsfilm had been superseded by the introduction of a smaller version of the 2-inch (51mm) videotape first used in a broadcast by CBS in November, 1956.

The tape revolution brought an end to the uncertainty of content and quality because, with the right equipment, the material could be reviewed on-site and, if necessary, re-shot. And it pushed back deadlines, because the material could be fed into programmes as quickly as the tape containing recorded pictures and sound could be rewound.

Electronic News Gathering (ENG) was – and remains – only one of the names used to describe the tape and new portable camera systems which went with it. In some areas it is called Electronic Journalism (EJ), in others Portable Single Camera (PSC). But users have never disagreed on one thing: the need for expertise on behalf of those who work with it. This is truer than ever before, because the watertight compartments which once separated the 'editorial' from the 'technical' are breaking down in the nineties, with the accent on economy of money and staff. The convention by which news-gathering was conducted entirely by skilled professionals, each independently responsible for camera, sound or lights, is giving way to the concept of single-crewing and multi-skilling. Small or non-unionized TV stations led the way, but now, even in the world's great news organizations, it is no longer heretical to suggest journalists should wield cameras, microphones, edit videotape, or camera-operators or sound recordists should be asked to write commentaries.

The effects are also being felt far beyond the professional user. Because the technology is simple to operate and continually improving in flexibility, reliability and robustness, almost anyone equipped with a one-piece camcorder is a potential source of raw material. Entire entertainment programmes broadcast in prime-time are now based on 'humorous' home video clips (many of execrable quality and taste), while 'Amateur Video' has become a familiar screen credit on certain types of hard news coverage.

To assess the impact on society of newsworthy home movie pictures it is not necessary to look beyond the events of May 1992, when riots erupted in Los Angeles after the acquittal of four policemen accused of beating up a black motorist. Graphic pictures of the beating were shot by an amateur, George

13

Holliday, who sold them to a local TV station for a few hundred dollars. The days and nights of death, arson and looting which followed the trial came as a direct response to what many believed was irrefutable evidence of police wrong-doing.

Another phenomenon is the 'Video News Release' (VNR), the audiovisual equivalent of the Press handout. The best provide useful, usable material for hard-pressed news organizations unable to cover events for themselves, but others – by accident or design – may give only a one-sided view. In the worst cases the VNR may be all that is on offer to journalists seeking answers to controversial questions.

14

At this early stage, the effects of single-crewing and multi-skilling on present-day professional standards of camerawork cannot be forecast with any confidence, because there is no guarantee that all who come to use ENG will be properly trained to do so or understand its full capabilities.

It is no concern of the authors who eventually comes to carry and operate the camera. The purpose of this book is to help ensure that whoever does so should also carry the expertise to use it well.

Towards a New Breed of Television Journalist

A place in the team

Sometime within the next few years, probably before the turn of the century, the fledgling profession of TV journalism will complete the ENG revolution. All the go-ahead news organizations will rely on a new breed of trained operator – neither traditional journalist nor technocrat, but a combination of both – who will be mobile and fully equipped to cover all but a small range of assignments requiring more than one person.

There is evidence that the halfway stage in the process has rapidly been reached: especially in local TV where there is close control over costs, it has become commonplace for a typical news-gathering team which once consisted of a journalist and up to three technicians (camera-operator, recordist and lighting assistant) to be reduced to only journalist and camera-operator.

The reporter leads

While the transition continues, expect units going on location to consist of the full complement, with a camera-operator and recordist taking instruction from the team leader – still identifiably an editorial figure (a reporter, producer or both where lengthier or more complicated events are concerned). The entire team may travel to assignments in a single vehicle specially adapted to take camera, editing and transmission equipment. In other cases, camera crews function independently of the reporter, with whom they rendezvous only to cover one assignment before being sent on to another. These camera crews usually carry sufficient portable lighting equipment to be able to undertake routine indoor work, and it is only when substantial areas need to be lit that specialist lighting assistants are called in. The team may also be joined by a facilities engineer to transmit the ENG picture and sound signals by satellite or microwave link to base, or by a picture editor, whose task is to assemble the raw material on the spot.

Reporter–crew relationship

Harmonious working relationships between the editorial and non-editorial members of the team are essential and may need to be worked on if any mission is to be successful. Although the reporter or producer is managerially in charge, the camera crew may have more experience in the field, and when this is the case they should not be inhibited about offering advice or guidance. Novice reporters sometimes mask their anxieties with shows of arrogance and awkwardness and may need careful handling until they learn more about the job, and teams should avoid personality clashes for the sake of their product.

 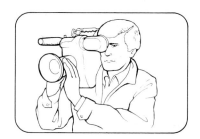

THE TRADITIONAL NEWS-GATHERING UNIT

Reporter, camera-operator recordist/engineer and (where necessary) lighting
assistant still make up the traditional news-gathering unit. But the size of the team
will have shrunk dramatically by the end of the century as technological
developments and cost-cutting lead to the acceleration of multi-skilling and
single-crewing.

17

News-gathering is Organized and Systematic

The news machine
News organizations in TV come in all shapes and sizes according to the status and the freedom of action they enjoy. The smaller they are, the more limited their sphere of operation, the more versatile their staff are expected to be, with little or no demarcation between editorial and technical responsibilities. Those serving national or international audiences may be staffed by hundreds of journalists, production and technical operatives, and although in parts of western Europe the trend is to encourage individuals to develop skills complementary to their primary activities (multi-skilling), more clearly-defined organization is expected and necessary.

News-gathering and processing
The basis of all effective factual programme-making is the organized sharing of responsibility between those who gather the raw material and those who process it. Experience has proved that each task makes different demands and calls for dedicated expertise. The separation is by no means always permanent or strictly defined, but it is hard to envisage a consistently successful news machine functioning under any other principle. Each arm has a name which accurately reflects its place in the system. Intake (otherwise known as Input, Assignments or The Desk) gathers the news and delivers it for Output to process and shape it for broadcast. So ENG camera teams, reporters, field producers and technicians belong to the news-gathering sector or Intake, whereas newsroom-based copy editors, writers, producers and studio presenters belong to the news-processing sector or Output.

Assignment planning
Rostered camera crews are assigned to stories by desk editors and planners at the end of an extensive, systematic process to filter items considered worthy of news coverage from the vast majority which are not. Outsiders are often surprised to discover that only a very small percentage of what is screened in any news programme is entirely unexpected. The rest is made up of coverage which has been undertaken as a result of previously gathered information, on the basis that camera crews have to be deployed before events take place if TV's appetite for illustration is to be satisfied.

Sources
This news 'agenda' is created from a wide variety of sources including official and semi-official reports, statistics, Government papers and discussion documents, other news organizations, internal and external *tip-offs*, and as a result of subscriptions to wire services. The *diary* is the depository for advance warning of potentially reportable political, commercial, sporting and social happenings of international, national or local importance.

News-gathering	News-processing
Long-term planners	Editors, producers and presenters
Assignments editors	Picture editors
Clerical support	Administrative assistance
Camera crews	Picture librarians
Reporters and correspondents	Graphics artists and designers
Facilities engineers	Studio production and technical staff

THE NEWS MACHINE

In big TV news organizations the responsibility for collecting the raw material and shaping/preparing it for broadcast is divided between two groups. Camera crews are an integral part of news-gathering 'Intake' or 'Input': presenters and editors belong to news-processing 'Output'. Smaller TV news stations may combine roles, but the functions remain essentially the same.

19

Your Contribution – One of Many Bricks in Programme Structure

The basics of factual programming

Despite the developments in technology and their noticeable effect on production fashions, factual programmes the world over tend to conform to one or a mix of formats limited by their editorial policy, duration, frequency and budgetary constraints. And however well or badly they are executed – whether they are brief bulletins hurriedly put together; painstakingly constructed programmes in fixed time slots for broadcast on a general channel; part of a 24-hour all-news diet; reporting matters of national and international gravity; bringing the audience's attention to local or regional events – the substance of what appears on the TV screen remains remarkably uniform.

Programme style

All are created from a small number of ingredients which have changed only in style and improved technique since TV news began to be taken seriously as a medium of information. The basics consist of live or recorded reports, interviews, graphics and items read by studio anchors, assembled in a way and to a duration which meets specific needs. So a weekly 'current affairs' programme, devoting its airtime to background analysis of the news, might choose to examine two or three subjects in depth or concentrate on only one through a single long report or interview. Alternatively it might present several contributions, each exploring different angles of the same topic. At the other end of the spectrum, a programme team might spend weeks compiling a feature for a monthly documentary slot.

The chain of command

Journalist editors or producers decide the composition of the overall programme, depending on their Intake (see page 18) colleagues or researchers for the logistical effort required to gather the material, and devolving responsibility for the separate segments to supporting editorial staff at base and to camera crews, correspondents and reporters in the field. So *your* contribution represents only one of many bricks in a complicated structure built for the sole purpose of getting that programme on air, and its fate depends on the whim of those responsible for shaping the incoming material to meet the demands of 'house' editorial style and programme duration. Other camera crews from your organization may be operating in parallel, all hurrying to meet the same deadline, and at any time the editor might decide to reduce or discard stories to meet unexpected changes in editorial priorities, or simply because the material fails to match up to the original expectations.

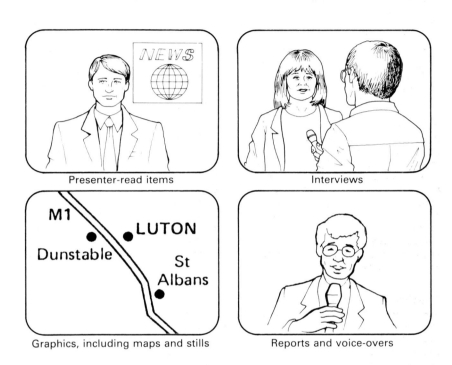

Presenter-read items

Interviews

Graphics, including maps and stills

Reports and voice-overs

NEWS PROGRAMME INGREDIENTS

Whatever their editorial remit and duration, TV news programmes comprise four basic ingredients: variety is lent by changes of style and emphasis. Differences between news organizations are chiefly those of item selection and treatment. The aim is to attract and retain viewers – especially important where audience size and appreciation are concerned.

From Colour Film to Videotape

The electronic revolution
For 20 years until the mid-seventies, the 16mm format dominated location work for TV news. In between, a few attempts were made to find alternatives, and there were some experiments based on the 8mm home movie format, but the proven versatility and flexibility of 16mm meant there were no serious rivals, especially after the introduction of colour film added an extra dimension to news coverage at the height of the Vietnam war.

Enter video
The next stage of development arrived in the shape of an entirely new approach. Videotape, emerging from its infancy, began to be seen as more than just a valuable tool for time-shifting, although the size, complexity and relative fragility of the equipment used to transmit and record sound and picture signals on to 2-inch (51mm) magnetic tape limited its benefits to studio-based production activity. But the path towards portability was inevitable, and the watershed was reached in 1974, when video cameras were used to cover the visit of American President Richard Nixon to China. Before long, broadcasters were vying with each other to replace their film cameras and processing equipment with an upgraded version of the U-matic video system used primarily for industrial purposes.
'Electronic News Gathering' had arrived.

ENG crosses the Atlantic
The first ENG recording was broadcast in Britain on 10 October, 1977. The subject was Margaret Thatcher, then leader of the opposition Conservative Party; the venue was her room in the House of Commons, and the cameraman — Bernard Hesketh.

The camera, a Philips LDK 11, was described as 'lightweight, compact and rugged, with a lightweight backpack'. It was fitted with three $\frac{3}{4}$-inch Plumbicon tubs and a 9.5mm to 95mm lens. The all-up weight for the cameraman was 18kg (40lb). The back-pack contained all the video processing circuitry, including contour enhancement. The manufacturers claimed that the picture quality would be acceptable after a two-minute warm-up period and would meet full performance specifications within 10 minutes at temperatures down to $-10°C$. The video and audio signals were recorded on the Sony 2859 HS VTR on the three-quarter inch (19mm) format.

All this was far removed from the modern ENG cameras and equipment described on page 45, but, in spite of a delay between the end of the experiment and lasting agreement with the broadcasting unions, for Britain it heralded the start of the ENG revolution.

CATCHING UP

Although ENG equipment was already in use in the USA and elsewhere, broadcasting organizations in Britain did not begin using it until the late seventies. The first ENG item shown on BBC TV News was an interview with Mrs Margaret Thatcher at the House of Commons on 10 October, 1977. Interviewer was David Holmes, Political Editor. Cameraman Bernard Hesketh is in the foreground (Courtesy of BBC Central Stills).

The Best Camera-operators are Newsaholics

News camerawork qualities
The best news camera-operators earn the respect and admiration of journalist colleagues for their ability to bring back pictures of good broadcastable standard under the most taxing of circumstances. But there is much more to it than sheer technical ability, and the main qualities may be summarized as follows:

Journalistic awareness
The best camera-operators are 'newsaholic' photo-journalists with a passion for their work. They do not just live off news, but are as good at setting the agenda as the editors they serve. They brief themselves on the way to a story, so they know what to expect. Once on location they are quick to understand the nature of the task ahead of them. The camera-operator learns to pick out leading political and public figures with unfailing accuracy: 'There is', says one experienced editor, 'nothing worse than being with a cameraman who takes little interest in the story, and who mistakes the Home Secretary for the local press officer, demanding to know where the nearest 13 amp socket is.'

Dedication
The cameraman/woman must be determined to get the very best pictures despite all obstacles. They need to be self-motivated and self-reliant, with faith in their own ability, and they must maintain their enthusiasm, even for the 'bread-and-butter' kind of story they have covered dozens of times in the past.

Physical fitness
Because they frequently find themselves in physically demanding circumstances when covering news events, camera crews must expect to be fit, though perhaps stamina is more important than sheer strength. Those who saw service during the 1991 Gulf War, for example, had to be able to put on life-saving protective suits against chemical and biological weapons within a short time. Crews in the front line were invariably younger – and male. The ability to do without food or sleep, perhaps for days at a time, is a precious quality.

Resourcefulness
Like their editorial counterparts, camera crews are judged by their success in carrying out their assignments. They are expected to be resourceful and persistent, not deflected by petty bureaucracy or logistical difficulties. In many ways this is the most fundamental requirement of all: the best camera-operators are of no use if they are unable to get their pictures – and deliver them back to base. In the hard world of TV journalism, you are only as good as your last story.

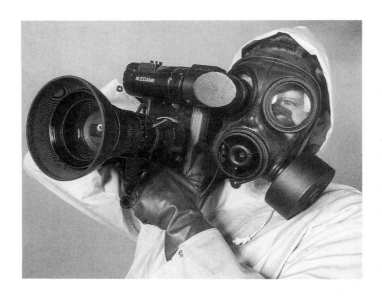

THE REALITY OF DANGER

Modern news-gathering is not for the faint-hearted. As a member of a camera crew you can expect to be called on to operate in dangerous areas which demand developed editorial judgement and common sense as well as physical fitness. The ability to be able to work effectively despite the encumbrance of specialist clothing including NBC (nuclear, biological, chemical) suits is a factor which has to be taken into consideration. (Courtesy of BBC.)

Make a Study of a Complementary Skill

How to make the grade

Don't believe anyone who advises you that the only way to 'the top' is by starting out sweeping the cutting room floor at the age of 15. Although it is of course still possible to begin at the bottom doing low-grade (low-paid) chores, anyone who is serious about making a career in broadcasting should first set their sights on the highest level of education. Journalism is increasingly a graduate occupation, and as the barriers between crafts start to crumble you should think of yourself as a member of that broader fraternity. The ideal mix would be some relevant academic subject – politics, economics, history, for example – plus some additional study to provide the essential background technical knowledge.

Multi-skilling

The value of familiarization with traditional journalistic techniques can also be demonstrated by the rise of multi-skilling, to which economically hard-pressed employers are turning with increasing interest. A working knowledge of some complementary technical skill, such as picture-editing, would also be worth gaining.

'Media' studies

Many British universities, polytechnics and technical colleges run what may be broadly categorized as 'media' or 'communications' courses. Some of these have well-deserved reputations for excellence, but there remains controversy within the industry about the value of others which concentrate on sociological and theoretical issues and offer very little practical work. If your ultimate goal is employment within the industry and you do decide on one of these courses, make sure you choose one which covers a range of study, including the opportunity to practise some of the basics.

For the aspiring camera-operator, successful completion of one of the recognized courses could be the first step towards qualification for a junior post in a TV or production company, some of which offer additional in-house or familiarization training, although few specialize in news and current affairs.

Other qualifications

Broadcasting is also one of the many British industries making concerted attempts to standardize vocational qualifications, and hundreds of freelances and staff from the major companies have devoted many hours working on the creation of levels of competence across a wide spectrum of occupational groupings. Among them are camera-work and journalism. The aim of these 'National Vocational Qualifications' is to increase the expertise of practitioners, with assessment in the work-place by experienced professionals.

The self-assessment chart opposite lists the major basic qualities required to be a news camera-operator.

Basic quality	Score		
	Yes	No	Maybe
	1	0	½
Appreciation of what makes good TV and cinema	✓		
Determination, patience and tact	✓		
Education to a good standard	✓		
Eyesight of the highest standard including colour vision	✓		
Foreign language ability			
Grasp of and liking for news, current affairs and politics			
Health and physical fitness			
Instinct for creativity	✓		
Interest in and understanding of photography and lighting	✓		
Natural scepticism			
Technical awareness	✓		
Quick reactions Totals:			

HAVE *YOU* GOT WHAT IT TAKES . . .

. . . to make a career of TV news camera-work? Check your own assessment honestly against the top dozen basic qualities required. Score under six and you should be looking for something else to do.

Perfect Composition with Stills or Home Movie Cameras

A talent for pictures

What sets good camera people apart from the rest is an ability to compose the picture in an attractive and interesting way even under the most difficult conditions in the field.

Stills photography

Many of the basic skills can be learnt and understood in stills photography, where modern equipment is cheap, light to carry and easy to use. It is an excellent way to start developing an eye for a picture, and the results of your work can be assessed and reassessed as you make progress. Looking through the viewfinder of a 35mm camera will provide the same aspect ratio as the current TV screen format (4 × 3), and will probably continue to be a useful guide to what can be captured on ENG until the next century when 16 × 9 becomes standard with the widespread introduction of High Definition Television.

Home video

The closest approximation to experience as a professional user of ENG is as a home movie-maker. Mastery of the equipment is likely to lead to requests to cover events for family and friends, with graduation, perhaps, to taking on weddings or anniversaries on a semi-professional basis. Advances in the development of domestic video equipment have now reached the stage where it is capable of really very sophisticated standards undreamed of by previous generations of amateur movie-makers who had to work on fiddly 8mm film cameras with clockwork motors. The frequency of 'Amateur Video' credits on news bulletins has become a clear sign of the progress that has been made and the ease with which professional news organizations can deal with the material, compared with the days when few had the facilities to process 8mm swiftly enough to take full value from amateur 'scoops'.

Video clubs

Access to one of today's highly sophisticated and good-quality camcorders will provide an opportunity to learn the grammar of picture-making, and to shoot in sequences rather than the single frames of stills photography. An alternative is to join a school or community video project or amateur video club. These exist in many towns, and anyone with genuine interest will find the experience extremely useful, especially if there is an opportunity to take part in collaborative projects where you can learn from others. At this stage the subject scarcely matters: simply understanding the basics will give you an insight into the effort which goes into the accumulation of well-composed and steady pictures.

SHOOTING STILL PICTURES

Looking through the viewfinder of a 35mm camera will give you the chance to compose pictures with almost the same aspect ratio as the current domestic TV receiver, 4:3. High-definition TV, with an aspect ratio of 16:9, will not be in general use until the beginning of the next century.

Amateurs are Spoiled for Choice!

Small formats
Home movie-making continues to be a popular hobby, and although film for amateur use is still available, the move towards video gains ground, with camcorder sales numbered in hundreds of thousands every year.

VHS-C and 8mm
Two small formats are available to the creative, news-orientated enthusiast, VHS-C and 8mm, which includes Hi8.

VHS-C (C for Compact cassette) tapes last 30 minutes and can be replayed on a standard VHS VCR using a special adaptor.

8mm, sometimes known as Video 8 and Hi8, will replay only on the appropriate machines, although the pictures can also be played direct from the camcorder through a TV set. With more than 60 camcorders in these formats currently available, the amateur is spoiled for choice. The high-band, top-of-the-range cameras provide the facilities needed for the best results. These weigh from about 1kg (2.2 lb) to 3.3kg (6.6 lb), the heavier models providing hand-held stability. It is, of course, also a matter of expense, and there are many low-cost cameras which perform well, providing good pictures and audio quality.

Before buying
Before buying, investigate the market, read the specialist magazines and if possible hire your main choice for a day or two to be satisfied that the camera is ergonomically right for you and has all the functions you are likely to use.

A taste of the top range
The following trio offer a taste of what is on offer at the top of the range:

Sony's Hi8 V6000E is one of the best-equipped, with many advanced features based on professional technology. It has impressive audio quality and RCTC – Rewrite Consumer Time Code – which can be recorded at the time of shooting or added later. A camera for the serious video-maker.

The Sharp VL MX7 8mm has a colour viewfinder, two CCDs and two separate lenses – a zoom 8 × 7 to 48mm and a 4mm 62-degree extra wide-angle primary lens.

Canon's EX1 Hi-Hi8 state-of-the-art camcorder, with its EOS EF 600mm lens, 2× extender and 2× electronic close-up function, provides an amazing 2400mm focal length. There is also a choice of interchangeable zoom lenses. With an adaptor ring, still camera SLR lenses can also be fitted, and as their effective focal length can be multiplied by five, they provide a considerable telescopic range.

THE GROWING POPULARITY OF AMATEUR VIDEO

A huge range of camcorders for amateur use is now available. Many, offering excellent quality and facilities, are manufactured by companies which also have a heavy investment in the professional market.

Learning to Live with One Employer

Up the organization – 1

The economic and social pressures which have created an environment for change in broadcasting have brought with them an atmosphere in which the number of those working for a single employer has declined. Indeed 'Skill Search', a survey commissioned by the main employers in Britain, showed that in 1989 a surprisingly high proportion of those engaged full time in the industry classed themselves as 'freelances'. The survey also forecast that the figure would grow along with the deregulation of broadcasting in the early nineties.

Staff crews

As conventions change, it has become unclear for how much longer the big international news organizations will continue to invest millions to recruit and retain top-class teams of camera crews on whom they can currently call to undertake a wide range of assignments. A roll of 30 or 40 two-person staff crews plus back-up technical staff is not unknown.

The need has been to ensure that commitments can be met effectively and quickly – if expensively. The most enlightened employers ensure that benefits include good basic salaries – often with premium additional rates of pay for unsocial or extra hours – membership of the company pension scheme, personal accident and health insurance cover, holiday and sick-pay entitlement, together with travel and duty expense allowances usually generous enough to allow crew members to live well during most assignments. On top of this they may be allocated the latest equipment, office cars and free protective clothing. In return for the security all this implies, the employers will expect to have hired loyal, dedicated professionals who will turn out to cover assignments at home or abroad whenever required and at whatever personal inconvenience.

On 'staff contract'

The next best thing to being on the established staff is being on a 'staff contract'. Here too the crew are providing their services exclusively to one organization. Many of the financial benefits may also be the same, with the chief difference being that these contracts are of a finite duration – a year, perhaps – which gives both sides the option of renewing, or not, according to circumstances. Contract crew members have to take care of their own pension arrangements and are usually paid more than 'staffers' to compensate. Depending on the employer, they may or may not have to provide their own equipment and transport.

The benefits of working on staff

- Good basic salary
- Allowances for working unsocial hours
- Company pension
- Accident insurance
- Private/company health care
- Regular paid holidays
- Sick pay
- Expense accounts
- Transport provided
- Latest equipment
- Availability of spares
- Technical and administrative support
- Free protective clothing

ONE OF A TEAM

In exchange for the security which goes with being employed as a full-time member of a large team, camera crews are expected to give their priority to calls on their time. Assignments may be difficult, dangerous or simply routine.

Favoured Freelances are Loaned Funds to Buy Equipment

Up the organization – 2

Some broadcasting organizations cannot afford or have no reason to employ full-timers. In many 'the news' is likely to be just another programme area to be served from a (usually small) pool of camera crews, and is considered to have no higher claim on an allocation of specialists than, say, drama or entertainment.

Freelances and stringers

Between the extremes of dedicated, expensive full-time staff and the often uncertain availability of generalists come the ranks of the ENG freelances. The highest status is bestowed on the regulars, who are given modest retainers to ensure first call on their services, and are then paid by the day or assignment. Others might be guaranteed so many days' work a year. The most favoured freelance crews might also be given loans at favourable rates with which to buy or replace equipment, which is far more expensive than basic film hardware used to be.

Some organizations, unable to justify the assigning of full-time staff, especially abroad, rely on freelances or 'stringers' to provide them with coverage from overseas bases, or subscribe to Reuters Television (formerly Visnews) or Worldwide Television News (WTN), the two leading international TV news agencies.

Some individual crews are employed on a contractual basis which allows them to work in collaboration with other news services (not usually direct competitors) so that operating, office and administrative costs can be shared. This is a principle which has been adopted by even some of the better off, who find the establishment of a foreign bureau much more economically acceptable if friendly international partners can be found. The same pool (shared coverage) principle may also be applied to specific assignments where the expense or danger of maintaining 'ownership' of a crew outweighs the desire for exclusivity.

Camera crew co-operatives

A growing phenomenon is the appearance of CCCs – camera crew co-operatives – in which like-minded freelances come together under one roof and continue to operate more or less independently while contributing something to common services. Even more recently, some staff crews – tiring, perhaps, of some of the inevitable bureaucracy which surrounds the bigger news organizations – have resigned to set up their own freelance pools, confident that they can undercut the competition on cost and still make more money than as staffers.

The trend is certainly away from huge teams of staff camera crews.

Worldwide Television News

Starbird Satellite Services.   TV Globo.
International Weather Productions (IWP). TV Asahi.
Focus Worldwide Television.   IRIB.
La Cinq.   CTV.

KEEP RIGHT

INTERNATIONAL PROVIDERS

Two London-based international TV news agencies provide coverage for TV
stations around the world through a network of strategically-placed camera crews
and journalists. Visnews, known as Reuters Television since January 1993, has
offices in more than 20 of the world's major cities and five regional bureaux in the
UK. Worldwide Television News, owned by ABC, the Australian Nine Network and
ITN, has more than 70 crews around the world and 14 overseas bureaux.

Freelances Enjoy Artistic and Ethical Freedom

Going it alone

The versatility of modern camcorder equipment makes it more feasible than ever for those intent on a career in news-related camera-work to operate on a freelance basis, either alone or as one of a team. As a freelance you enjoy the artistic and ethical freedom to accept or reject assignments as you wish – benefits you may be denied as a member of staff with a big organization, where you can expect to have job security in exchange for an existence controlled by others.

The appeal of freelance work

This freedom is a large part of the appeal and satisfaction of freelance work, especially for those whose experience is too limited to interest employers, or at times when staff openings for beginners are few. Roaming the world to cover assignments of your choice sounds a romantic and exciting alternative. But there is a down-side.

Coping with the practicalities

Setting up as a freelance needs careful thought and a proper business and financial strategy. First of all no news organization of any worth is going to accept your work unless it meets its requirements, which are likely to be stringent. ('Hot' news coverage is of course an exception, but no freelance beginner can expect to be in the right place at the right time often enough to be able to make a career out of such events.) So forget the lucky one-off scoop and, before you do anything else, consider the following fundamentals:

- The potential market
  - decide whether it is geographic, generic or specific
  - identify style and typical content
  - identify typical duration
  - identify regularity
- The commissioners
  - make contact with editors/producers/commissioners
  - confirm that freelance contributions are accepted
- Your contributions
  - assess whether you have saleable ideas
  - decide if you can execute them to likely editorial and technical requirements
  - decide whether you can sustain a viable service
- The competition
  - confirm existence
  - decide whether you can compete effectively
  - decide whether the market can support more than one freelance
  - compare your strengths and weaknesses
- The decision
  - decide whether sufficient opportunities exist
  - assess whether you can make a living

- Office accommodation (and local taxes)
- Telephone
- Heating
- Lighting
- Furniture
- Equipment (e.g. pager, fax, computers)
- Administrative support
- Camera equipment and spares
- Equipment maintenance
- Car
- Insurances (car, equipment, health, travel)

THE COST OF GOING FREELANCE

Going freelance involves a heavy financial burden (see list above) unless you can be sure of a ready market. A basic camcorder and accessories could cost in the region of £35 000 (mid-1992 prices) or approximately £250 a week over three years before any interest charges are taken into account. Most freelances' lives are dominated by securing assignments and raising the finance for equipment, so setting up a co-operative with other professionals could be the ideal way to share costs and maintain some of the camaraderie of the camera crew room.

A Freelance must Exude an Aura of Efficiency and Reliability

Financing freelance work
Assuming the prospect of even modest success, going freelance implies a willingness to undertake the same huge personal, organizational and financial commitment which goes with the establishment of any business. It is not a recommended pastime for the faint-hearted. There is more to it than the ability to wield a camera effectively: if you hope to be taken seriously, you must first exude an aura of efficiency and reliability, so a list of 'musts' would look something like this:

Office accommodation
A suitable base is needed, with access to ordinary office furniture and facilities: telephone, fax, typewriter and photocopier are probably the minimum requirements. It is possible to work from home, but this should be regarded as only a temporary expedient unless it is unavoidable or arrangements can be made to convert and equip a spare room. A telephone-answering machine is also a very useful modern tool, but probably less so than some other kind of human message-taking service.

Equipment
If you expect to freelance on a regular basis you need equally regular access to reliable camera equipment, accessories and spares. Hiring is possible but is likely to be prohibitively expensive for all but the most dedicated. Outright purchase would probably be a better long-term alternative, with a loan – assuming the availability of acceptable collatoral – adding to the financial burden.

Transport
Once you have the camera equipment, you need something to transport it in when on assignments. Stowing it in the boot of an ordinary saloon may be good enough: more likely you will need a bigger, sturdier model with decent locks to deter thieves. A car phone and fax machine will also be valuable if you want to keep in touch with base.

Miscellaneous
Unless you are genuinely working as a single operator, chances are you will need to team up with at least one other person to share the responsibilities, even if not on every assignment. So you will need to find and employ a reliable recordist or lighting assistant (electrician) for which there may be an agreed union rate. Car, equipment and health insurances will also add to the outlay. So will protective clothing and footwear for dirty and physically difficult jobs; and smart wear for covering formal events. Fending for yourself will include arranging travel, sorting out passports, passes and permits for events, and scores of tiny administrative details. And remember: time spent queuing for a visa or negotiating car-parking space is time lost on the road.

Expect to Settle for Routine Assignments Early On

Freelance in operation
Once you are in business, it is a matter of deciding how you are going to work, and for what rewards. Freelance camera-work can be a lucrative as well as satisfying business for those at the top of a crowded profession, but as a beginner attempting to break in you must expect to have to settle for routine assignments and standard rates of pay until you prove yourself.

Daily and assignment rates
The work of 'real' freelances, as opposed to those on contracts of finite durations, is inevitably governed by the outlets they serve. Daily newscasts are likely to employ by the day, longer or less frequent programmes by the assignment. A typical 'daily' user will pay a scale rate for a set number of hours, organizing the schedule so that the same crew is able to cover more than one event. ('Second jobs' are notorious for being covered just to make more use of a crew who would otherwise go off duty after half a day's work.)

How much?
As a beginnner you may expect to have little room for manoeuvre. Very impoverished programmes or stations may be in no position to pay anything more than token amounts, but unless you are desperate to see your material on the screen they are probably best avoided in the first place. Rates of pay for work undertaken on behalf of reputable organizations are usually determined during negotiations which take place periodically between representatives of the biggest employers and the recognized trade unions. 'Above-the-rate' agreements depend on the experience and reputation of the crew members and the type of assignment being covered. Established freelances find it advantageous to be paid in a way which allows them legitimately to offset the cost of their equipment against income tax, asking employers to make a definite distinction between paying for the professional expertise and for what in effect is the 'hire' of equipment whose purchase has been financed by bank or other loans. 'Extras', such as overtime, travel expenses, meal allowances, the use of additional or specialist staff and equipment and so on, are subjects for separate agreement.

Getting your money
However honest and reputable they may be, even the biggest organizations are not always efficient in the way they handle freelance payments. Accounts procedures can often be maddeningly slow, and as a freelance you should always make a point of finding out what documentation is necessary, whether supporting evidence (travel and meal receipts, for example) is required, and to whom it should be submitted. It is invariably worth getting to know the people involved in a department you deal with regularly, as the friendly personal touch may well aid the speeding of a cheque in your direction.

The Basics of Camera Operation

Getting to know your camera

Before you can expect to be an effective camera-operator, it is essential to have a thorough understanding of how the equipment works and what it does. Don't rush into it: read the maker's manual carefully and try to absorb the basics. Many features are common to modern professional types, but for the sake of example we will take the Sony BVW 200/300/400 series, considered the market leaders in the early nineties.

First steps

- With the tripod adaptor (base plate) secured to the tripod head, slide the camera along the front groove until it locks into position. *Always* check that it is well anchored.
- Fit and connect a charged battery into the battery case at the back of the camera, and switch on. Check the viewfinder to ensure that 'humid' is not displayed. Press the ejector button to insert a cassette, ensuring that the window faces outwards.
- Adjust the viewfinder, moving it left to right, backwards and forwards until it feels natural and comfortable.
- Adjust the eyepiece to suit your eye. Point the camera at a distant object, such as a building with regular vertical and horizontal features, set the lens to infinity, then rotate the eyepiece dioptre adjustment ring until you have a truly sharp image. Alternatively, switch on the colour bar generator and adjust the dioptre ring to get a sharp raster.
- With the colour bars still displayed, adjust the brightness, contrast and peaking controls to get the best display. Fine-tuning may be necessary when viewing the first correctly-exposed picture.

Setting the black balance

Put the gain selector switch to 0 and put the output/DCC switch to CAM. Push the spring-loaded AUTO W/B switch to black and watch the adjustment progress in the viewfinder. When the BLACK OK appears, allow the switch to return. The red, green and blue BLACK LEVELS will now be set. The iris will close automatically during this sequence. If the lens is not in the AUTO mode it will have to be opened manually for the White Balance.

Setting the white balance

Select the FILTER to match the lighting conditions. Set gain switch to 0 and output/DCC switch to CAM with the WHITE BAL selector to A or B, and put the lens in the AUTO iris mode. Place a white card or object in front of the light source. If, as so often happens with news events, there is a mix of light, ensure that the 'white' is angled to and reflecting the light from the main source. Zoom in close on the 'white' so it fills approximately 80% of the screen. Push the AUTO W/B switch to WHT. The adjustment will take about a second. The viewfinder display will indicate WHITE OK.

Now both black and white balances will be stored in the memory.

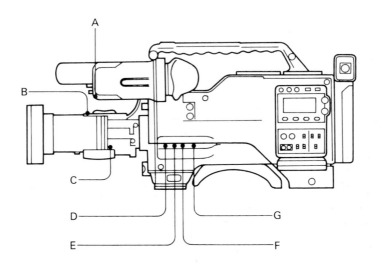

TYPICAL ENG CAMERA CONTROLS

A: Audio Indicator Switch
    In the 'on' position, audio channel one is indicated in the viewfinder. In the
    'off' position there is no indication.

B: Iris

C: Zoom

D: VTR Power Switch
    Reduces power consumption in the 'save' position.

E: Gain Selector
    Increases gain to video amplifier from 0db to 9 or 18db.

F: Colour Bar Switch
    To switch in colour bar generator.

G: White Balance
    Allowing memory storage of different white balances in positions A and B.
    Preset, a factory setting, provides a white balance of 3200K with the filter
    selector in position 1 and 5600K in the other positions. Use this option when
    there is no time to change black and white balance.

If You're Not Sure What a Function Does – Don't Use It!

Setting the shutter

In most situations you will not find it necessary to use the electronic shutter, which – as with a stills camera – is supplied to improve the clarity of fast-moving objects. But if you are unsure, don't use it.

To set the shutter, switch from ON to SEL (SELECT). The speed, in this case 1/100, appears in the viewfinder display. While the colon on the left of the 'SS' appears, each depression of the switch will advance the speed to the next value. Although the intensity of fluorescent and mercury lamps appears constant, it is flickering (oscillating) at 50Hz (60Hz in the USA) and is disturbingly apparent at fast shutter speeds.

Setting the time code

Move the REAL TIME switch to SET. Set the correct time with the SHIFT and ADVANCE buttons, then put the REAL TIME switch to ON and the time-coding will begin. Because it is powered by a tiny, built-in lithium battery, timing will continue even during battery changes.

Time code is converted to video information and recorded on lines 19 and 21 of the 625-line PAL picture. This is factory set, but adjustments can be made to put it on a limited number of other lines in the vertical interval blanking period (this is the gap between the two rapidly interlaced 'fields' which go to make up a TV picture).

Video gain

Video gain – 9db and 18db – should be used only in poor lighting conditions, as indicated in the viewfinder display. Both increase the 'noise' level (the grain structure of the picture), 18db to an almost unacceptable level. Video gain can, however, be a life-saver when shooting at night or under really poor conditions.

Dynamic Contrast Control (DCC)

To be activated when shooting against a brightly lit background or a scene of stark contrasts. The iris should respond to the light on the subject. The use of DCC, in conjunction with the advice on page 52 should greatly reduce these problems.

Audio

Switch on the DOLBY NR noise reduction system when using oxide tapes (the system works with metal tapes, regardless of the switch position). With the supplied microphone mounted on its camera bracket and connected to the mic input socket on the front of the camera, set the audio recording level. This microphone should be used only to record ambient sound.

Before shooting . . .

The camera is now ready, but before shooting record one minute of colour bars at the start of a fresh tape. This will allow engineers to assess the quality of the camera's video information.

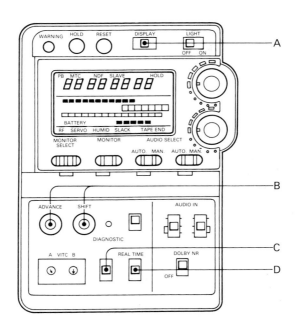

CAMERA SWITCHES

A: Display Switch
    Changes counter display to show Tape Running Time (CTL); Time Code
    (TC); User Bits (U-Bit) (any additional information which can be recorded on
    the vertical interval or control track).

B: Time Code Start and Advance Buttons

C: F Run/R Run Switch
    F Run to set the time code by real time or to lock the built-in time code
    generator to any external time code source; R Run – time code moves only
    in the record mode.

D: Real Time (time of day) Switch
    On – to record real time in VITC; Off – not to record real time in VITC; Set –
    to set real time.

The Growth of Video for Amateur and Professional Use

The development of video since its introduction in the early fifties has resulted in a range of sizes and qualities. The main ones are:

Betacam
Developed from the amateur BETA standard for the professional ENG market. Its six video recording heads, compared with BETA's two, produce a far superior picture quality. BETA SP (Superior Performance) is an improvement on BETACAM. It uses metal particle tape to increase picture resolution and has four heads for each Y (luminance) and C (chrominance) channel. The finer structure of the tape enables the use of higher carrier frequencies, enhanced bandwidth and signal-to-noise ratio. In use by many TV news organizations.

Video High 8
Developed by Sony. Uses an 8mm videotape, rotary two-head helical scanning system producing pictures of broadcast quality. Considered by many to be the format of the future because of its lightness and ease of operation.

Half-inch VHS (Video Home System)
Developed by the JVC company. Produces good pictures for the domestic consumer but is not aimed at the professional market.

Half-inch S-VHS
S stands for Super or Separate. A semi-compatible component* recording system rather than a composite system to an amateur/professional standard.

Half-inch M format
An upgraded component VHS system using six video heads, recording at six times the standard VHS speed. Adequate for industrial/professional use.

Half-inch MII
An improved M format with enhanced bandwidth and recording times.

Three-quarter-inch U-Matic
Now semi-professional, the workhorse system of the early years of ENG. Largely superseded by BETACAM SP.

Other formats
Quadruplex (quad): the first broadcast standard video format. It used two-inch tape. Four heads recorded transverse tracks at 90 degrees to the direction of tape travel. No longer manufactured. One inch: a standard video format used chiefly for studio work; 19mm DI: a component digital system; 19mmDII: a composite digital system; Half-inch DIII: Panasonic's composite digital system.

* Component video is a signal in which the luminance (Y) and the chrominance (C) signals are recorded separately. Composite video combines the luminance and chrominance signals by encoding.

(1)

(2)

VIDEOTAPE FORMATS

Magnetic videotape records sound and vision signals. In less than 40 years, tape size has shrunk from 2 inches (51mm) on bulky quadruplex reel-to-reel machines (1) to half-inch (13mm) in compact videocassette recorders (2). Broadcast-quality 8mm tape is already in use. (Courtesy of the BBC.)

The Camera Aims to Emulate the Delicate Movements of the Eye

The grammar of film and video
As grammar is basic to the use of language, so a grammar of film and video has evolved over the past century to aid the use of visual communication, and to allow the camera to extend the sense of human vision beyond its natural limits. What you are trying to achieve with the camera is the emulation of the delicate ease and precise movement of the eye.

The static frame
This is where the camera does not pan, tilt or zoom. Always use a tripod. Treat the frame in the way a journalist writes a sentence, conveying the maximum information succinctly. That means not wasting space: convey only relevant information and include, where possible, movement and activity in order to avoid producing a still picture.

   The static frame is the simplest and easiest way to communicate. It should not be so wide an angle that detail is unclear, or so close that vital information is excluded.

Perspective
A picture which shows a subject in isolation can mislead: the viewer may not comprehend its size. Introduce a familiar object to give more accurate perspective. A hand adjusting a vase, for example, will be an indicator of true size.

Static shooting of activity
When shooting vibrant activity – bustling streets, motorway traffic, civil disturbance in which missiles are being thrown and crowds running riot – try to encompass the action in the static shot. Undisciplined, aimless panning and zooming makes the viewer uncomfortable, sometimes causing a feeling of disorientation, rather like car sickness, and is anathema to the picture editor. A moving subject must be allowed to move into and out of frame. Don't switch off in mid-shot: it may leave the editor with no choice but to make an unacceptable jump cut. Frame shots to maintain consistent exposure throughout. If a picture has a correctly exposed foreground and an over-exposed 'burnt-out' background, the background detail will be lost.

Documents and papers
When shooting these, make allowance for the slow reader. As a guide, read the relevant passage twice to yourself before switching off. The reporter could help the viewer by speaking the extract as part of the voice-over. In situations where 'hand-holding' is the only option, keep your body well balanced, with legs slightly apart, to ensure your static shots are steady. Take advantage of any extra support, such as a wall or lamp post, for added stability.

46

(1)

(2)

PERSPECTIVE

An article shown in isolation (1) may give no clue as to its size. Putting a hand into the picture (2) helps the viewer to comprehend.

Panning Needs Careful Planning

Panning
Panning is the horizontal movement of the camera, with or without the tripod. It is a much-abused technique because it is often either unnecessary or poorly executed, and it consumes screen time as well as inhibiting editing. So first consider whether a static shot would serve better. Once you have committed yourself:

- rehearse the movement
- start with a static frame shot of at least three seconds
- end with a static frame shot of at least three seconds
- don't over-pan to include unnecessary distractions
- pan slowly enough to let the viewer take in the picture information
- pan fast enough so that screen time isn't wasted
- record pans at two speeds to allow the reporter more freedom in writing to the picture
- pan left to right and right to left
- avoid panning over scenes where there are big changes in light levels
- as with the static shot, don't waste frame space

Panning (hand-held)
Stand with legs apart and point the camera in the direction of the pan without moving your feet. If they are together you restrict the arc through which you can turn as well as reduce stability.

Tilting
Tilting is the vertical equivalent of the pan: the guidelines above apply.

Zooming
Intelligently used, the zoom is formidable. It makes for perfect framing and rapid changes in focal length, plus, of course, its zoom facility. As with the pan, the zoom should start and end on a static shot of at least three seconds. In fact, in general terms, the rules of panning apply equally to zooming. Your lens may have a focal length range of 8.5mm to 119mm, i.e. a ratio of 14 to 1. Most lens-makers provide a doubler, which requires just a flick of the lever to increase the focal length to 238mm, with a light transmission loss of about two stops. With focal lengths of that order, the camera requires a very firm base, and great care is needed when panning and tilting.

The macro
The macro enables close-up coverage of small objects, such as postage stamps, to fill the screen. The operation is quite simple on most lenses. Pull out the macro lever and rotate the ring fully in the direction of the arrow. Then rotate the focusing ring until it contacts the stopper on the M.o.D side. Move the object (or the camera) to get the required picture format. Precise focusing can be achieved by adjusting the zoom control.

48

(1)

(2)

(3)

(4)

MAKING BEST USE OF YOUR SPACE

Aim to fill the frame to its best advantage. There is too much empty road and not enough factory in illustration 1 and the closer shot (2) is far better. Similarly, the road in the foreground (3) contributes nothing to the information offered to the viewer. Illustration 4 is far less wasteful of space.

Careful Framing will Eliminate Under- or Over-exposed Areas

Exposure and lighting

Given normal eyesight you will be able to see detail in a very poorly-lit object, where the reflective light index is one foot-candle – the amount of light covering an area one foot square and one foot from the candle. Simultaneously you will be able to see detail in an object with an index of 1000 foot-candles. That means the human eye's ability to take in the contrast between the darkest and brightest object is in a ratio of 1000 to 1. The best film stocks have a contrast ratio in the order of 100 to 1 and the best video cameras cannot separate detail in reflected light measuring a ratio of more than about 35 to 1. So it is important always to bear this limitation in mind when shooting with a video camera.

Overcoming lighting problems

With careful framing it is possible to eliminate areas in which the detail would be markedly under- or over-exposed. If they are essential to the coverage, shoot them separately, making allowance for the extra time you will need for accurate framing and exposure.

In general, the rule must be to avoid shooting directly into the light source, whether it is natural or artificial. Where this is not possible, use artificial light or a reflector as a means of achieving balance.

Your main aim, at all times, is to create an even, natural look which will not distract the viewing audience.

Landscapes

Pictures of a landscape, taken looking into the sun, can enhance detail and improve separation and clarity, creating an attractive, three-dimensional effect. Artistic use of back-light – natural or artificial – can also make fine pictures. But keep the light off the lens, as the resulting iris pattern can be intrusively offensive.

An adjustable matte box will be extremely helpful here in keeping out unwanted light as well as protecting the lens from rain or dust.

Including humans

Human figures may be included in a landscape but they attract attention out of all proportion to the space they occupy, so ensure they fit naturally into the scene and are not on a scale big enough to become the main interest. As a rough guide, if it is possible to see the expression on a face, that person will become the subject and the picture will no longer be a landscape.

Towns and cities look unnatural without people, but don't let the people steal the picture if your aim is to portray the town.

50

MATTE BOX

An adjustable matte box fixed to the front of the camera will keep out unwanted light and also protect the lens against rain and dust. (Courtesy of OpTex.)

Golden Rule: Use Just Enough Light to Ensure Quality Pictures

Exposure guidelines

To expose a picture correctly, make sure the zebra pattern generator is switched on to provide the video level display. Adjust the iris ring until the display just disappears from the highlights or flesh tones of the picture.

Iris operation

Given a choice of automatic or manual iris operation, experienced operators will always opt for control of exposure – they always have the choice of switching to automatic in confirmation. They also become used to tracking changes in light levels by adjusting the control as they go along, for while the auto iris provides accurate exposure in most conditions it cannot discriminate in 'rogue' circumstances.

For example, imagine you are shooting an interview in a busy street. The auto iris is giving you a perfectly correct exposure until a large, white high-sided lorry moves slowly behind the interviewee. The auto iris will then 'lock on' to the white expanse, reducing exposure, and until the lorry has passed out of shot the interviewee's face will be grossly under-exposed. Conversely, if it had been a dark lorry there would have been an unacceptable increase in the exposure. (Remember the contrast ratio factor.)

Using artificial light

The golden rule here is to employ just enough light and lamps consistent with producing quality pictures. The use of too many lamps complicates the task, creates more shadows, uses extra power and can be overwhelming to people who are unused to facing the camera. Remember also the extra physical effort involved in carrying extra lights – an important detail if you are working alone or are a long way from your transport.

Interiors

When shooting in a room where there is a predominance of daylight, fit your lamps with full blue gelatine or dichroic blue filters. The 5600K camera filter will also have to be used. The blues will reduce light levels by about two stops. But the best advice is to try to avoid shooting interviews against a window where there is a marked imbalance of exterior to interior light. The face will be properly exposed but will be overwhelmed by the exterior natural light, and remember that activity through a window could also be distracting.

Other problems

Dark skins should not present problems if very light backgrounds are avoided. Probably one of the difficulties is lighting to avoid reflections from spectacles. It may be enough to alter the camera angle a degree or two, but it is more likely the subject will need to be lit more from the side, with the lights raised. It's a situation in which you can't always win.

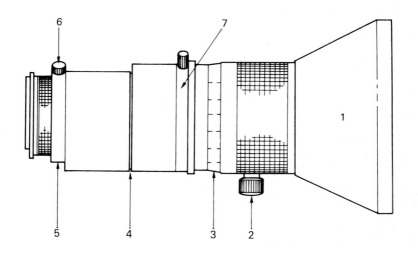

LENS OPERATIONS

Some of the main working parts of a typical ENG zoom lens.
1: Lens hood
2: Focus ring
3: Zoom ring
4: Iris ring
5: Macro ring
6: Macro lever
7: Index line

Using a Back Light Will Help Reveal Character

Lighting an interior interview
A typical one-to-one interior interview can be shot very effectively with two lights, each of about 800W. One is positioned as a back light to provide separation and modelling in order to avoid the 'deadpan' look and reveal the interviewee's character. This light must be suitably 'barn-doored' to keep the light off the lens. The second – key – light should be close to the line of the camera and on the opposite side to the back light. The interviewee should also be close to that line on the same side as the back light.

Three-light set-up
Where a three-light set-up is preferred, the back light should be opposite the key light and the third used as a softer fill light. Use barn-doors to confine the light and to help eliminate unwanted flares (flares can also be overcome by simply adjusting or moving an object, for example slightly opening the door of a glass-fronted cupboard or changing the plane of a glass-fronted picture by propping a matchbox behind it).

Lighting backgrounds
The background is usually adequately lit by the light of a two- or three-lamp arrangement, but this would not be enough when shooting in a large room or hall. The problem can be overcome by concentrating a 2kw lamp on the background, but if you have nothing more powerful than 800w, simply move it closer to the background to maintain relative light levels. It may also be necessary to reduce the camera angle to keep the lamp out of shot.

For an extended interview, arrange the lighting so the background is very dark compared with that on the subject's face. This requires skill in setting the lamps and barn-doors, but is worth doing to help audience concentration.

Providing duality
Some camera-operators will work only in available light, however inadequate, in the pursuit of 'realism'. That may be fine for documentaries, but it is generally not an acceptable option in news, so in the absence of a sufficient level and quality of natural light, it is necessary to provide whatever artificial help is needed to give the picture a 'lift'. The use of 9db or 18db of gain increases picture noise level.

Under-exposed pictures look flat and lack detail, and seem worse when intercut with better material. A politician seeing unlit, poorly exposed coverage of his own interview followed immediately by well-lit, well-exposed pictures of a rival will understandably be aggrieved. This sort of imbalance is unacceptable: the rule is to light to a high standard wherever possible.

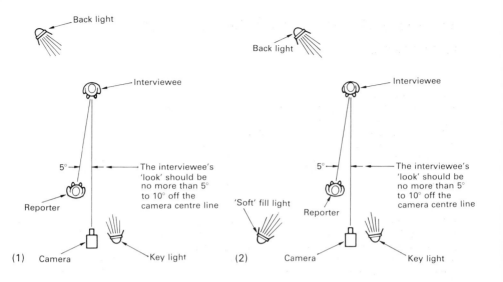

(1)

Back light

Interviewee

5° — The interviewee's 'look' should be no more than 5° to 10° off the camera centre line

Reporter

Camera   Key light

(2)

Back light

Interviewee

5° — The interviewee's 'look' should be no more than 5° to 10° off the camera centre line

'Soft' fill light

Reporter

Camera   Key light

(3)

LIGHTING AN INTERVIEW

1: Two-lamp interview set-up.
2: Three-lamp interview set-up.
3: Portable lighting kits can range from 300 to 800W and are extremely effective for illuminating interior news-style interviews (see page 58). (Courtesy of ARRI (GB) Ltd.)

Battery Lighting is Ideal for the In-car Interview

Lighting equipment

Although ENG crews generally carry a smaller range of standard lighting equipment than the specialist 'sparks' who worked with comparable newsfilm teams of the past, the introduction of modern technology means that on most assignments there is virtually no measurable difference in effectiveness or quality.

The battery light

The battery light remains an essential piece of equipment for any ENG crew, and is most suitable for in-car interviews and the ubiquitous night-time piece to camera. The modern variety, made of non-conductive materials, is safe, lightweight and durable, and provides an even distribution of light from optimized reflector shapes and surfaces. A barn-door, safety glass, a dichroic* blue filter, a diffuser and spare bulb compartment in the handle are standard fittings for the 100W range offered typically by Sachtler of Germany. It is powered by a 12V, 4.5Amp/hr battery, which will keep the light going for 30 minutes. The 7A/hr version will power the lamp for 1 hour, or 30 minutes when sharing its energy with the camera. With the correct adaptor, the battery charger can be powered from a 12V car supply via the cigarette lighter socket.

The light distribution measured at five metres is 800 lux[†] full spot and 200 lux full flood.

The HMI (metal halide discharge lamp)

This gas discharge light source has been in use for many years, offering high levels of luminance at 5600 degrees Kelvin and greater efficiency than tungsten. Its drawback is that it requires a very high initial voltage – 30kV – to create an arc (i.e. a luminous discharge) to excite the gases in the bulb. A ballast unit provides the very high voltage, a mains protection circuit and the lamp's relatively low operational supply.

The HMI battery light will deliver more than twice the light distribution at a daylight colour temperature to that of a similar wattage tungsten source. It also dispenses with the dichroic blue and its attendant two-stop filter factor loss.

The similar, more powerful 250W Sachtler doubles the light distribution over the same distance, and there are also 20W and 50W very lightweight lamps, providing excellent light distribution, which are ideal for mounting on camera or lamp-stands.

---

* The dichroic blue filter changes the tungsten colour source from 3200K to the daylight 5600K.

[†] Lux is the illumination per square metre of surface at a distance of one metre from a point source of one candela (roughly the light from one candle).

(1)

(2)

THE BATTERY LIGHT

An essential piece of equipment for any ENG camera crew. (1) The modern,
lightweight variety offers a range of power operated by a 12V battery. (Courtesy
of OpTex.) (2) The advance of single-crewing has led to the development of
camera-mounted lights.

Low-wattage Lightweight Units Help Reduce Freight Charges

Mains lighting
A kit consisting of three portable lamps, housed in a purpose-designed flight case big enough to take all the accessories, should be adequate to provide the mains lighting levels required by camera crews undertaking routine news assignments.

These lamps are available from a wide variety of manufacturers and range in strength from about 300W to 800W. For the freelance, who cannot call on extra lighting, it would be advisable to buy the equally efficient, higher wattage lamps needed to light larger areas. Size and wattage are not the only criteria. Many small, well-designed lamps produce light levels equivalent to those nearly twice their wattage and size. Compare manufacturers' light distribution figures, quoted in lux, with the lamp in both the spot and flood modes. The crew which travels regularly by air would probably prefer the low-wattage, lighter weight units to help reduce freight charges.

Accessories
Standard accessories, if not already part of the original kit, should include, for each lamp:

- safety mesh
- safety glass
- two or three scrims (diffusers)
- barn-doors
- dichroic filter
- compact lightweight stand
- cables with plugs
- 110V and 230V lamps (bulbs)
- a selection of plugs to match alien sockets

Reflectors
Reflectors are used mainly by ENG crews to correct any imbalance that results when only one side of an interviewee's or reporter's face reflects a high level of sunlight, creating an unacceptable contrast with the other.

The typical 95cm (38-inch) reversible silver/white reflector folds into three concentric circles, reducing it to a third of its original size, and is suitable for news work. The white side reflects a soft light, the silver a harder light with optimum reflectivity.

Lux and foot-candles
They may seem complicated, but these are the only two measurements of light you will come across in ENG. How many lux you need to expose a picture depends on the sensitivity of the charged coupled devices (CCDs) in the camera and the speed of the lens. As a rough guide, take the range, 600–1000 lux, or 56–93 foot-candles without the use of video gain. As an example, the Sony BVW 300 AP camera lens can be stopped down to f8 at 2000 lux to expose the picture correctly.

USING A REFLECTOR

A reflector is very useful outdoors on those occasions where it is necessary to balance the strength of natural light, especially as it affects skin tones.

59

Pictures Without Sound Lose their Impact

Shooting sound

It is surprising sometimes how little emphasis is placed on the effective use of sound – speech apart – in the coverage of news. For while the commercial cinema spares no expense to post-synchronize dialogue, and lay extra effects and music tracks for dubbing to a high standard to complement the pictures precisely, programmes intended to mirror reality often neglect the extra dimension offered by the microphone.

And although the days of silent-only coverage may have disappeared, to those who would still say of a routine assignment 'there was no sound' it is worth pointing out that silence does not exist. Natural sounds occur even in the quietest moments of modern life. Machinery hums, traffic rumbles, floorboards creak, humans cough, birds sing, insects buzz, wind whistles.

Shooting 'wild track'

Do not overlook the fact that pictures without good sound lose their impact. Always think of them as complementary elements, never one without the other. Aim for continuity, which may mean extending the length of your shot to help sound editing. Never switch on too late: never switch off too soon. If the circumstances in which you are working are such that audio coverage is fragmented, shoot a 'wild track' of the ambient sound which can be used to overlay the whole sequence.

Do not expect the 'archive' to come to your rescue: some news organizations question the ethics of using material not recorded contemporaneously.

Reflecting sound reality

Sound should reflect the reality of the situation. If you know your reporter is going to say 'all hell is being let loose', make sure the sound supports his words accurately. It is disconcerting for a loud explosion to sound like a popping cork. Anticipate: switch off the auto volume control (AVC).

Music

Shooting any group of musicians or singers presents a difficult task, especially as you may normally expect to have no control over them or their performance.

- Your priority is to shoot a general view with a master sound track consisting of a complete tune, or at least a substantial passage, as an aid to editing.
- If possible, ask musicians to repeat a passage to allow you to shoot close-ups and mid-shots. Avoid finger and arm movements that make synchronizing difficult or impossible. Shots playing sustained notes, close-ups of vibrating strings or heads of instrumentalists, will edit in successfully if carefully framed.
- With vocal groups, after the completion of the master, shoot reverse angles and audience reaction as cutaways. And if you shoot a close-up of the music score, make sure it is the one being used: someone is bound to notice if it is not.

SHOOTING MUSIC

A master wide shot of the whole ensemble will provide a context in which you should be able to concentrate on closer shots of sections or individuals. Avoid finger and arm movements which would make synchronism with the sound difficult or impossible.

The Camera-operator's Eyes and Ears in Dangerous Situations

The recordist
To the experienced camera-operator working for any of the world's leading news organizations, going on assignment without a recordist would have been professionally and technically unthinkable until a very few years ago. The only single-crewed teams were those who operated out of small-time or non-union television stations, or who were stationed in very remote areas. Under normal circumstances the occasions when a top camera-operator went solo were restricted to the need to shoot 'mute' pictures.

But as single-crewing becomes increasingly widely accepted as the norm in news-related TV programming, there is a danger that the craft of the specialist recordist will be lost. Those who remain should be valued even more highly.

The recordist's main duties
In addition to his or her own professional skills as an audio engineer, the recordist should be sufficiently experienced to deputize for the camera-operator or, when there are two cameras in the unit, to provide back-up coverage. But it is also fair to say that the recordist is often the junior (and younger) partner who aspires to the higher status of camera-operator. During this unofficial apprenticeship the recordist is expected to 'pull focus', share the burden of equipment-carrying and set up the camera in the required modes, whatever the situation, so releasing the camera-operator to investigate story details. In dangerous situations the recordist acts as the eyes and ears of the team, watching out for trouble while the camera-operator, absorbed in the task of picture-taking, has vision and audio senses limited by the closeness of camera to face. Similarly, during a walking shot, the recordist can guide the camera-operator clear of obstacles. The morale engendered by the successful combination of camera-operator and recordist, especially in difficult conditions, cannot be overestimated.

Other aspects
There are other aspects of the recordist's many duties, all of which should be interchangeable with other members of the crew. These include:

- choosing the correct microphone for each task
- ensuring a cassette is always in the recorder, ready for use
- arranging for the despatch of completed tapes
- acting as a 'fixer' and decoy, for example engaging officials in conversation while the camera-operator continues with the coverage unhindered
- driving and/or navigating and parking the camera car so that other members of the crew can immediately go to the story location
- carrying out all routine field maintenance on equipment.

In addition, some understanding of basic picture-editing technique is a useful skill for the recordist to acquire.

THE RECORDIST

An essential member of the crew in his or her own right. There is more to the job than choosing the correct microphones and balancing sound levels. As the practice of single-crewing gathers momentum, more recordists are graduating to the level of camera-operator.

Wind Shields Should Always be Available for all Microphones

Microphones
An understanding of the characteristics of all types of microphones used in ENG coverage will help the camera-operator or recordist in making the right choice to match operational requirements. Where possible always use a wind gag (shield) on every microphone.

Clip-ons
The clip-on microphone is very small, unobtrusive and ideal for in-shot interviews and pieces to camera. It requires only low-voltage power supply with batteries which have a life of up to 6000 hours. This omnidirectional Electret microphone has a flat extended frequency response. The polar diagram gives an indication of a typical omnidirectional response. News-related programmes now accept that these tiny microphones can be in shot rather than hidden under clothing, ensuring the sound is not muffled.

Directional or gun microphones
The directional qualities of this specialized microphone depend on its length and design features. The perforations along the length of the tube introduce phase cancellation of the sound waves approaching from the side, so being sensitive in one direction only. The main drawback of the design is its weapon-like shape, which can draw unwelcome attention to the user.

Cardioid
These are so-called because they absorb sound in a heart-shaped directional pattern and can be moving coil or condenser in design. They have a front reception area of about 160 degrees and are especially suitable for recording music.

Condenser
The condenser is essentially omnidirectional. Some are designed with two diaphragms and can be switched to change the polar characteristics through bidirectional to cardioid.

Hand (stick) microphones
These condenser, cardioid phase-cancellation microphones, with their interference tube, provide high-frequency directional characteristics, with good separation from ambient noise, especially when held close to the mouth. The stick mike, usually about 250mm in length, is very popular with reporters, as it requires very little preparation and can be ready for use within a very short time.

Lip microphones
Noise-cancelling ribbon lip mikes, traditionally used by sports commentators, are held as close to the upper lip as the mouth guard will allow. The high-frequency response characteristic with a marked cut-off at about 7000Hz provides good voice quality, while reducing high-frequency ambient noise. Lip microphones are also very useful for reporters doing voice-overs in situations which demand an absence of background sound.

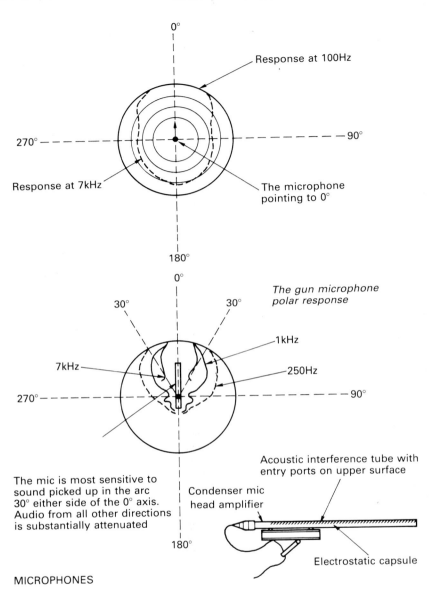

0°

Response at 100Hz

270° — 90°

Response at 7kHz

The microphone pointing to 0°

180°

0°

The gun microphone polar response

30°   30°

1kHz

7kHz

250Hz

270° — 90°

The mic is most sensitive to sound picked up in the arc 30° either side of the 0° axis. Audio from all other directions is substantially attenuated

180°

Acoustic interference tube with entry ports on upper surface

Condenser mic head amplifier

Electrostatic capsule

MICROPHONES

The directional response of a microphone is represented by a polar diagram where the mike is at the centre. A perfect omnidirectional mike would have a circular diagram. In practice it is not quite circular, except for the low frequencies, but at the higher ones it picks up sound equally from all directions. Personal/neck and some hand mikes have this characteristic. The Sennheiser ME-K3U stick microphone has a similar cardioid lobar response to retrieve even the quietest passages. It has a transformer-balanced XLR output and a bass cut switchable in two steps. A useful ENG microphone.

Don't Expect Radio Mike Reception Round Corners

Radio mikes
The radio microphone has become one of the essential tools of modern-day reporting. It frees the speaker from the camera in a way which can never be achieved with a microphone lead, allowing much more variety of coverage. Radio mikes have been in use for many years, but early versions had a reputation for unreliability.

The transmitter/microphone is no larger than a hand mike – some 200mm long by 20mm in diameter – but in the right conditions can deliver sound with a frequency response of 50Hz to 15Hz, indistinguishable in quality from that produced on a microphone line. The range at which the signals can be received are influenced by body absorption, the proximity of buildings, metal structures, trees and shrubs, so it is wise to expect the best reception within the line of sight between transmitter and receiver over about 150m. The receiver is about the size of an average cigarette packet.

Radio mike advantages
The main advantage of the radio mike is the ease and speed with which it can be placed at distance from the camera. Gone are the days when great lengths of cable were used to cover press conferences in large halls. The mike also offers the journalist almost complete freedom when performing pieces to camera or walking interviews. It can be used as an RF link between the camera and the recordist's sound mixer, effectively removing the mixer/VCR umbilical cable and giving the crew independent movement at the same time as maintaining control over sound levels and equalization. This has become particularly useful since trouble-makers learnt that one way to interrupt camera crews at work was to cut the cord between operator and recordist.

Frequencies
All RF circuits should be checked carefully before shooting to ensure there is no interference from another source. Most countries allot frequencies/channels for use within their own borders. The manufacturers match these frequencies, so their equipment will operate perfectly well unless troubled by a rogue transmitter. Before taking a radio microphone abroad, seek the advice of someone who has experienced similar assignments.

The aesthetics of microphone use
Sound – usually speech – accounts for more than half the essential information in a news item, and news and current affairs programmes demand that every word is as audible as circumstances allow. Ideally, no camera-operator wants the microphone in shot, but if it becomes unavoidable no matter: always remember that aesthetics takes second place to the story.

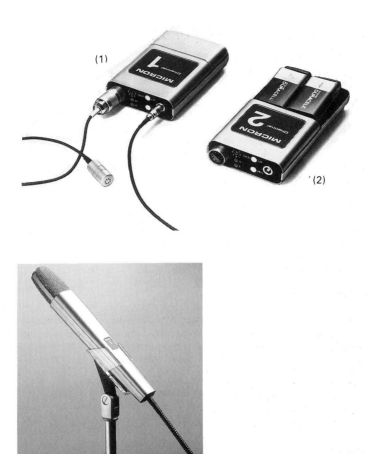

(1)

(2)

(3)

RADIO MICROPHONES

Radio mikes, once notoriously temperamental, have become an essential tool for both interior and exterior locations, freeing the reporter from the restrictive microphone lead. Shown here: Micron's TX 100/500 pocket transmitters (1) with personal mike connector (2). The TX 100 measures 93 × 62 × 22mm (3.7 × 2.4 × 0.86in) and weighs 235g (8.1oz). The TX 500 measures 120 × 62 × 22mm (4.6 × 2.4 × 0.86 in) and weighs 290g (10 oz). The TX 503 hand-held transmitter/radio mike (3) is for use with 500 series receivers.

67

Be Equipped to Make Use of Pool Sound Feeds

More about sound
Rather than conduct individual interviews or make a series of separate announcements about some newsworthy event, a growing number of organizations of all types call news conferences with the aim of reaching the widest possible broadcast and press audience at once.

Pool feeds
Depending on the location and the time they need to set them up, organizers of these news conferences sometimes provide sound pool feeds from distribution amplifiers (DAs), one purpose being to avoid the demands of those wielding a forest of microphones. Some news conferences are held at the same time and place as a matter of routine, so allowing familiarity with the technical requirements, but the output terminations from DAs can vary widely, so do go prepared with a range of plugs, sockets and jacks to match their outputs.

Other microphones
Gun, neck and hand mikes should be plugged into the two XLR audio input sockets mounted on the back of the video recorder. A switch immediately above the sockets will supply phantom power if needed. Audio level controls, auto/manual switches for both channels, are to the right of the Time Code display window. There is also a facility to monitor either channel or a mix of both and to monitor playback simultaneously while recording or E to E (electronic-to-electronic) to monitor direct.

The audio mixer
As the camcorder is a combined audio/video recorder it does not provide the professional recordist with all the flexibility she or he requires. For example, at the exact moment the camera operator makes a quick pan, the recordist needs to make a marked adjustment to the mic control level, but cannot do so without the possibility of disturbing the camera movement. The result is that the sound is not of the quality it should be. So the audio engineer turns to the mini-mixer, where it is possible to have continuous control over mike and line inputs, with a measure of equalization.

A number of very small, lightweight professional three-channel mixers are available, offering microphone powering, peak metering, peak limiter and off-tape monitoring facilities. There are also stereo mini-mixers for recordists who need to work in true pan-potted stereo or twin-channel mono. They are well engineered, with every combination of channel switching and monitoring circuits for decoding the stereo signal.

Although news broadcasters generally have yet to adopt a stereo system, it may pay the freelance who covers both current affairs and other assignments to invest in a stereo system in anticipation of future needs.

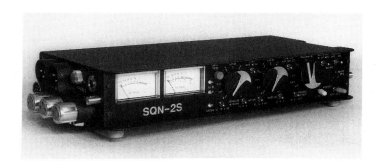

THE AUDIO MIXER

The SQN-2S miniature stereo mixer (Courtesy of OpTex). Although TV news has in general yet to adopt stereo sound recording, any freelance expecting to take on other assignments as well as news may find a stereo mixer system a worthwhile investment.

New Demands on the Picture Editor

Stereo

Stereo technology, bringing to sound reproduction a sense of enhanced quality and reality, has been popular with music lovers for more than 30 years, but it was only in 1991 that terrestrial stereo TV was first made available to domestic users in the UK.

To receive these broadcasts, viewers needed to be equipped with NICAM (Near Instantaneously Companded Audio Multiplex) TV sets or recorders. The success of its CD quality has added another dimension to home viewing.

Thousands of stereo TV programmes have been produced, based on established and evolving microphone and recording techniques, but for a variety of reasons news broadcasters have been slow to take up the challenge. One of the main drawbacks is the extra demands stereo sound recordings will place on the picture editor, who is already under considerable pressure to shape the raw video material in time for bulletins.

Stereo in the field

Technically, stereo presents few problems for the ENG operator in the field, for whom matters can be simplified by the use of the coincident or stereo microphone. In this unit, both microphone capsules are in the same housing, as close to each other as possible. In this configuration, the audio signal reaches both microphones at almost exactly the same time and they will consequently be in phase with each other. The differences in level will be the result of their directionality; this is called the M (Mid) and S (Side) technique.

The M, mid-microphone, should be pointed at the centre of the sound source. The S, side-microphone, must have a figure-of-eight polar pattern and have its positive recording axis pointing to the left of the audio source at a right-angle.

Signal channels

The coincident pair reduces the need to use separate microphones, and therefore cable runs, to create the desired stereo effect. It has a five-wire, five-pin output socket. Its cable is divided into two three-pin XLRs as inputs to the camcorder or stereo mixer, the M signal being recorded on channels 1 and 3, the S signal on channels 2 and 4 on the Beta SP system. The digital format Panasonic DIII offers four independent tracks, giving more flexibility. Camcorders are not yet equipped for stereo monitoring, so although the operator will hear the M signal in the left headphone and the S signal in the right, this is not true stereo. A video cassette modification, combining a small matrix circuit plus stereo socket and headphones, will provide true stereo monitoring, which is also available using the SQN 4S or AD260 mixers.

As you will gather, stereo recording is complex enough without the demands of the visual image. If possible, attend a special course on stereo; Focal's *Single Camera Stereo Sound*, by John Ratcliff and Neil Papworth, is also required reading.

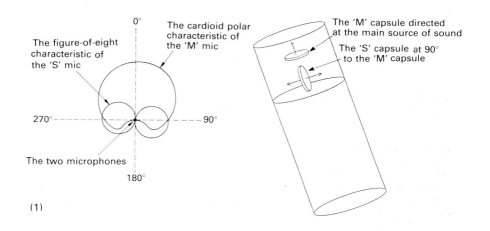

The figure-of-eight characteristic of the 'S' mic

The cardioid polar characteristic of the 'M' mic

The 'M' capsule directed at the main source of sound

The 'S' capsule at 90° to the 'M' capsule

0°

270° — — — — — — — 90°

The two microphones

180°

(1)

(2)

STEREO

1: Characteristics of coincident pair stereo microphones.
2: Sony ECM-MS5 stereo microphone. (Courtesy of Sony Broadcast & Communications Ltd).

Make Sure Your Camera Fits Your Needs – and Your Pocket

Buying an ENG camera

Investing in ENG equipment is a serious and expensive business, and any freelance contemplating such a move would be well advised to take a number of factors into consideration before making a final decision.

Choosing your format and line standard

First choose the format to match the demands of your potential market. The wide choice includes Betacam, Betacam SP, MIII, D3 and Hi8. Then comes the standard in which to operate – PAL (Phase Alteration by Line), the 625 50Hz system used widely in Europe: NTSC (National Television Standards Committee), the American 525-line 60Hz system, or SECAM (Séquentiel Couleur à Mémoire) used by France and Russia. Signals from these different systems are incompatible unless fed through a standards converter and will affect your ability to serve a range of organizations.

Camera configuration

For the freelance confident of his or her market, a dockable camera is preferable to the one-piece with integral video recorder. Dockability means flexibility, because the recorder can be replaced by an adaptor which allows operations with a free-standing recorder or linked and electronically locked to other cameras in a studio or outside broadcast situation.

A camera with a Hi8 back as well as Betacam is also worth considering.

Focal length requirements

The choice of zoom lens will almost certainly be decided by focal length requirements. Doubler and macro facilities are usually standard. There is a wide choice of speeds and focal length (see page 76).

Viewfinders

The camera should also have the facility to mount a 5-inch (127mm) or similar viewfinder, so useful in sports, outside broadcast and studio coverage. In these situations zoom and focus remote controls are also needed for mounting on the tripod pan handles.

Other facilities

These include

- state-of-the-art CCD technology with extreme sensitivity to give high-quality pictures at low light levels
- electronic shutter to capture clear images of high-speed motion
- genlock capability for use in multi-camera operations
- auto iris function
- black and white balance memories
- viewfinder displays to indicate most camera functions (recording status, audio and video levels, white and black balance confirmation, filter, gain and shutter speed settings, etc.)
- phantom power available to external microphones
- nickel-cadmium batteries and charger (essential)
- a.c. adaptor camera power unit (very useful optional extra)

72

1. General appearance
Look for obvious signs of wear, tear and rust. A sparkling, clean camera may indicate it has been well looked after: it may, of course, disguise major faults.
2. Missing parts
Make sure no parts of the camera or accessories are missing.
3. The chip block (CCD)
Connect the camera video output to a proven monitor, cap the lens, and with the maximum gain, contrast and brightness, look for white holes in the black picture. Black holes indicate a failure of pixels in the CCD. A white hole would indicate a failure of a block of pixels. If this appears in the centre of the picture, this would be unacceptable. Frame a high-contrast picture (e.g. a dark scene with a lamp in shot), then over-expose about two stops. Accentuated vertical smear or star effects near the light, plus loss of detail in the less well-exposed parts of the picture would make the camera suspect.
4. Black level
With maximum gain switched on and off, observe the black level difference in the picture. The only visible difference should be the extra noise (graininess) when at full gain.
5. The VCR
Record colour bars and replay on a studio VTR which is time-based corrected. Compare colour matching with the camera video output. Watch for head drop-out. With a high-contrast picture look for possible black tearing on the highlights. Test Record, Fast Forward, Rewind, Play and Eject functions using fresh tape. Between each test remove tape to check for damage.
6. The lens
Make sure front and back surfaces are unmarked. Check the back focus to ensure the correct setting is not at the extremes of the adjustment. To ensure lens tracking is precise, focus critically on a building with regular vertical or horizontal features. Check sharp focus by zooming slowly through the whole focal range of lens. Check that auto-iris responds speedily to changes in light levels and that a smooth change is effected by the motorized zoom. The VCR switch mounted in the lens should have a clean, positive action.
7. Viewfinder
May age prematurely; should provide a sharp, balanced picture.
8. Audio
Record and replay a variety of sounds on a proven system.
9. If in doubt . . .
. . . check with an experienced camera engineer.

BUYING SECOND-HAND

What to look for in used equipment.

The Camera-operator is Spoiled for Choice

Predicting change

Television news organizations agonizing over a choice of camera equipment spend considerable amounts of time trying to forecast future technical developments which could make what they buy rapidly out of date. Such is the speed of change, a wrong decision could cost millions.

For the freelance dependent on the broadcasters for a living, the actual amount may be smaller but proportionately just as significant. It is not many years since those who bought U-matic equipment found that all too soon those they were serving had switched to Beta SP, and the value of their purchases slumped.

Predicting changes in news formats has become more difficult than ever, the only certainty being that the broadcasters will opt for smaller, lighter weight equipment consistent with quality, along the lines of the Sony Hi8 system. Then there is the increasingly accepted digital format. Ask your main clients what plans they have, and buy accordingly. As an interim measure investigate the second-hand market, but have each unit thoroughly checked by a qualified engineer.

Camera types

At the time of writing, the Sony Beta SP was considered to be the market leader in professional ENG equipment, with its BVW 200/ 300/400 series one-piece camcorder. The BVW 300 AP weighs 7kg (15.5 lb) complete with viewfinder, battery, cassette and lens, and its refined ergonomics make it comfortable to use, providing good peripheral vision for the operator. The HL V55 is the Ikegami company's one-piece camcorder, which has an additional Hyper video gain setting of 30db. Sony, Ikegami and other manufacturers produce dockable cameras which can be used as camcorders. The Sony BVP 7A camera with the BVV 5/5PS video-cassette recorder, or with the CA 50P camera adaptor, for use in a multi-camera operation, and in such a dual role, could be financially rewarding for the freelance.

Digital format

The world's first half-inch digital camcorder, the D310, was launched by Panasonic. The digital format has been developed to overcome the loss of picture quality which plagues analogue video recorders during editing and dubbing. In other words, it eliminates generation losses. Even in the analogue formats, video signals are frequently processed digitally, only to revert to analogue. The D310 offers a range of facilities similar to its analogue counterparts. The Hi8 format could 'take-off' as the broadcasters' choice for the future. Sony's very lightweight EVW 537P, using 8mm videotape, incorporates many of the features of its half-inch big brothers and still provides excellent quality.

74

THE SHAPE OF CAMERAS TO COME?

The Panasonic AJ-D310 D3 digital camcorder. The digital format has been
developed to overcome the loss of picture quality during editing and dubbing.
(Courtesy of Panasonic UK Ltd.)

Protect Your Lenses with Ultraviolet Filters

Lenses

Lenses for ENG cameras come in an almost endless variety. They range from the 180-degree fisheye to the telephoto long focal length primary lens, plus all manner of wide-angle attachments, and extra-fast and periscope snorkel systems for underwater coverage. These are specialist lenses and would not be part of your normal equipment, but it is as well to know what is available to meet the requirements demanded of an exceptional assignment.

It takes time to investigate and hire (or buy) the right equipment, and specialist suppliers exist in most countries versed in film-makers' needs. There you can expect to find items such as the Schwem Gyro-Zoom FP1, which features innovative optical and electronic engineering to stabilize images and remove vibration, making it possible to shoot close-ups confidently from 300m (1000ft), even when on board boats or aircraft. If you can anticipate the need for sustained coverage of this nature, it is worth the cost of hire. Purchase at early 1992 prices would be upwards of £12 600.

Standard zooms

The demands imposed by the disciplines of news coverage are well-served by the flexibility and quality of more readily available standard zoom lenses.

Canon, for example, make an 11m $f2$ to 363mm at $f3.3$. With the built-in ×2 extender it continues to 726mm at $f6.6$. They have also designed a practical ENG range, including the 18:1 zoom (8.5mm $f1.7$ to 153mm $f2.3$ with ×2 extender) and the 14:1 zoom (8.00mm $f1.7$ to 112mm $f2.1$ with ×2 extender). All lenses incorporate a macro system for close-up shooting.

A variety of zoom accessories screw to the front of the lens: among the most useful is the Telephoto Converter, which can substitute for the built-in 2× converter but does not incur its 2f stop light loss. The Wide Angle converter can zoom through the entire focal range, whereas with the Wide Angle Attachment the macro lever is used for focusing, making the zoom inoperable.

Lens protection

Whatever your system, protect your lenses by fitting ultraviolet or similarly factor-free filters. Also, when you are not using your lenses, keep them capped against scratches. Repairs are more costly than filter replacement. If, despite all your precautions, the lens does become so damaged it is impossible to focus with any combination on the zoom and focus scale, by framing your shot and adjusting the macro lever you should get a reasonably sharp picture, though it will not be possible to use the zoom.

You will of course need to re-focus in the same way every time a change of focal length is required, but this technique may be enough to get you out of trouble in an emergency.

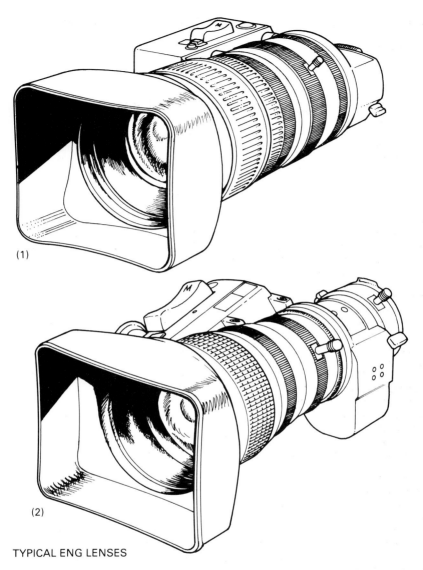

(1)

(2)

TYPICAL ENG LENSES

Modern technology offers an excellent range of lenses through a variety of manufacturers. Those shown are typical examples of what is available. The Canon J 33A (1) has an exceptionally wide zoom range with high performance levels to meet the stringent demands of the CCD camera. With the introduction of internal focusing, the colour aberration and corner performance changes have been markedly reduced. The square hood offers protection from rain and unwanted light, but would not be as effective as a matte box.

The widely-used Canon J 14 (2) is one of a range with remote focus and zoom controls mounted on the tripod pan-handles. These facilities are invaluable for sports and studio coverage.

Hand-held Coverage Should be Your Last Resort

The tripod

The professional uses a tripod whenever circumstances permit. Hand-held coverage should be considered only as a last resort. A tripod is an important piece of equipment: ensure what you use is good enough to do the job properly. It should also be ergonomically right for your personal use. Every adjustment should be instinctive, as if changing gears when driving. The more intuitive the mechanical part of the operation, the better you will be able to concentrate on all the other aspects of picture-gathering.

Tripods in use

A good professional tripod, made of metal, carbon fibre or any other substance, must be of sufficient weight to give you steady pictures when panning and tilting with your usual lens complement. The head should have a built-in spirit level and the legs should be extendable. Other important points to note are:

- A heavier, more substantial model providing an extra secure base is needed when using very long focal length lenses.
- If the tripod legs are extended you will need to stand on something solid so your eye is in line with the eyepiece and you have easy access to all the camera and tripod controls. Standing on tip-toes to try to see through the viewfinder will create difficulties of movement as well as being uncomfortable and tiring.
- The position of the tripod legs is not always important, as long as the camera is secure and steady.
- When covering any event which requires panning through 180 degrees, place the tripod legs so you can move through that arc with ease. It is essential to be able to keep your balance when executing this kind of shot. Rehearse it whenever possible.

Monopods

A monopod is a sturdy, telescopic metal pole which screws into the bottom of the camera. It is lighter than most tripods, while providing some support. Its drawback is that as it cannot stand alone it offers less versatility than the conventional tripod. Supapod is a lightweight version, complete with integrated friction head. Its versatility allows it to be used as a tripod substitute, and it can be transformed to become a brace. An adjustable cross-strap is slipped over the left shoulder and the pod drops into the socket. The four-part telescopic tubes open out to give a lens height of 182cm (72 in). Closed, it measures 61cm (24 in) for use with the brace.

Baby legs

This is a very small tripod, invaluable when working at or close to ground level and in confined spaces.

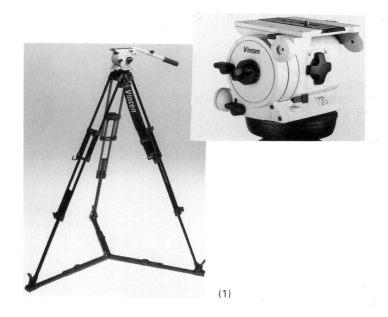

(1)

(2)

TRIPODS

A steady picture is one of the basic principles of ENG camerawork, so always use a sturdy tripod whenever possible.
1:   Vinten 20 tripod with pan and tilt head (Courtesy of Vinten Broadcast Ltd)
2:   Sachtler Baby Legs for use at close to ground level (Courtesy of OpTex)

A Revolution in the Language of Camera Movement

Specialist equipment
In addition to the standard equipment carried by most crews on routine assignments, a very wide range of accessories has been developed to meet specialist needs, leading to the growth of an army of manufacturing suppliers. The following represents a small sample.

Steadicam
Like all truly great inventions, Steadicam has the virtue of simplicity. The system is designed to free the camera from the constraints of the tripod and at the same time to eliminate the extraneous movement associated with hand-holding. It provides mobility, portability and versatility, while allowing the recording of steady images. It allows the camera to move with the operator as if it were an extension of the body and part of the human internal gyro servosystem, automatically adjusting and correcting body movements when shooting over rough ground; crossing thresholds; walking up or down steps; doing long walking (tracking) shots and shooting from moving vehicles, including aircraft. Steadicam has revolutionized the language of camera movement, earning its inventor both an Oscar and an Emmy in recognition of its contribution to the film and television industry.

There may be times when you would wish to take advantage of the system, but do not hire a unit without engaging a well-experienced, specially trained operator.

The Mutterbox
Television reporters frequently have to provide reports by telephone some-times minutes before – sometimes during – news programmes. Unfortunately telephone quality is not always of the best, particularly in remote parts of the world. It is now possible to remedy this problem by using a 9V battery-powered amplifier and inserting it into the telephone circuit to raise the voice or tape-recording closer to broadcast standards.

The 'Mutterbox', as it is known, is mono-stereo compatible and allows for two-way conversation/interview between the reporter in the field and home base. The unit is provided with a variety of plugs, sockets and leads to connect with modern and older telephone systems. It also comes with details of all the many types of connection you are likely to encounter. The Mutterbox weighs 240g, is the size of a packet of twenty cigarettes, and is very easy to use. In addition to the standard model there is also the more sophisticated and larger desk-top version, which includes an audio mixer.

But take care: in some parts of the world tinkering with telephone circuitry to insert the amplifer might be frowned upon.

(1)

(2)

SPECIALIST EQUIPMENT

Steadicam (1): a revolutionary piece of equipment which gives the camera operator the freedom to be mobile while keeping the picture steady. (Courtesy of Steadicam).

The Mutterbox (2): enhanced sound quality over telephone circuits. (Courtesy of Gavan E. Kelly Ltd).

You Have No Story without Charged Batteries

Batteries – your lifeline
It is surprising how often new or inexperienced camera recruits, while happily ticking off an impressive list of the creative and technical requirements needed for effective news-gathering, manage to overlook the importance of battery power. They have to be reminded that the day will come when they will be assigned to a war zone or a remote area where the mains supply has failed or is unreliable, and then they will understand the value of that every ounce of energy from their batteries. And the key to achieving that is by care, maintenance and correct charging.

Superfast charging
Manufacturers say the active working life of ENG batteries can be increased by 1000% and simultaneously re-charged faster than ever before, thanks to new technology. Re-charging from flat can be measured in quarters of an hour rather than the hours or days of not many years ago, and there are also systems which will operate from a car's 12V d.c. supply and deliver usable power to a battery within a very short time.

There are four elements in the superfast charging programme:

- initial pre-charge checks
- a main fast charge
- a balancing charge
- a maintenance charge

Superfast charging can bring a battery back to full power in about 30 minutes. It takes between 20 and 45 seconds for state-of-the-art chargers to check the state of the battery electronically. The current applied is a special pulse train, part of which depends on the response of the battery. If it is not fully charged it will receive the superfast charge; batteries already fully charged are not damaged – they receive just the controlled maintenance programme to bring them to peak condition. The system will also reject batteries with serious faults. As the fast-charge cycle is complete, the balancing charge segment begins. This supplies a series of special current pulses to bring each cell simultaneously to full strength. The maintenance charge ensures that each cell is also protected, so one is not deeply discharged while the others maintain their levels.

Storage
When a battery is being properly charged it will stay cool, and when it is overcharged or charged too quickly it heats up. High temperatures cause permanent damage to the battery's chemistry, reducing its capacity and life expectancy. Batteries should not be charged at temperatures of 0°C or lower, or stored at high temperatures. They are complex pieces of chemical engineering and if well-treated will give long and faithful service.

Remember: without charged batteries you have no story.

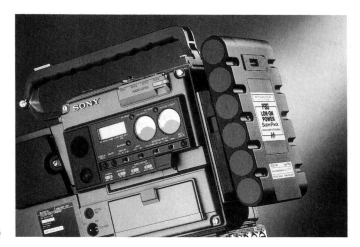

(1)

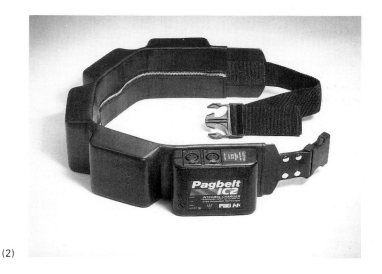

(2)

YOUR LIFELINE

The importance of looking after your camera battery cannot be overstated. It is
your only hope when mains power is unreliable or absent. Examples: (1) PAG
battery on a Sony BVP 50 camera. (2) PAG battery belt can be used to power both
camera and fill light simultaneously. (Courtesy of PAG Ltd.)

83

Damp and Dust – the ENG Camera-operator's Biggest Enemies

Maintenance

Modern ENG camera equipment is generally well-made, reliable and robust, and as such can be expected to withstand a certain amount of the mishandling which is an inevitable part of the hurly-burly of regular news-gathering. When breakdowns do occur, crews working for big news organizations will usually have access to repair workshops and a reasonable stock of spares. For the more modestly equipped freelance lacking such luxuries, each day the camera or recorder is out of commission is a day's potential income lost.

Use only qualified engineers

To reduce the likelihood of breakdown, have equipment regularly maintained and aligned by a qualified engineer. Lens tracking, pre-set colour balance, chrominance and luminance levels, and sync and line pulse levels, should be checked; tape path and video and audio heads thoroughly cleaned. Following a few other basic guidelines will also contribute to the longevity of equipment.

Basic maintenance

- Keep all camera equipment clean, with particular emphasis on the lens and viewfinder.
- Damp and dust are the camera-operator's biggest enemies, so make sure all panel screws are secure.
- If rain is forecast use the maker's waterproof cover. Failure to protect the camera has cost some crews dearly in unnecessary maintenance costs and wasted time.
- Check all the video camera functions, preferably viewing the results on a colour monitor.
- Battery protection is a worthy subject on its own (see page 82). To avoid damage, don't discharge nickel cadmium batteries deeply before re-charging or leave them shorted out for extended periods. If lead acid batteries are used, refer to the manufacturer's charging instructions.
- Maintain cables and connectors in good condition. Have a spare supply.
- Establish a routine check of all items and functions which are rarely used to ensure they remain in working order.

CAMERA MAINTENANCE

Modern ENG cameras are robust and reliable, and will give years of reliable service, but will last longer if properly maintained. To reduce the likelihood of breakdown have your equipment checked by qualified engineers in recognized camera workshops.

Advertising Your Presence May Not be a Good Idea

The camera car

The fictional image of the TV news camera car, emblazoned with identifiable company logos, screeching to a halt at the scene of some major incident is mostly best left where it belongs. Vehicles carrying satellite or microwave dishes are of course bound to be noticeable, but what the professional crew seeks more often than not is the anonymity of an unmarked estate car, station wagon, minibus or large saloon with heavily tinted windows. The reason is that ENG vehicles identified as such are alas too often the target of those who would find your presence unwelcome. But always be prepared to put a programme or channel symbol on the windscreen when you know it will help your passage or parking.

General requirements . . .

Any camera vehicle you employ should be big enough to carry a three-person team – camera operator, recordist/engineer and reporter – and to conceal all the equipment. Locks and alarms should be sturdy enough to deter all but the most professional thieves. The vehicle should be able to cope in all weathers and road conditions, with a four-wheel drive facility. Some means of communication with home base is also essential, and more and more vehicles are equipped with portable fax and computers as well as mobile telephones.

. . . and the essentials

Regard the equipment list below as the minimum for carrying on the camera vehicle. A list of auxiliary equipment is shown opposite.

Video	Audio
Camcorder and/or camera and recorder	Audio mixer
Videotape cassettes	Microphones (two lavalier-type,
Batteries	one gun, two cardioid, plus
Battery charger	their windshields)
A.C. adaptor – mains unit	Floor and table mike stands,
Tripod and camera mounting plate	mike boom, mic cables XLR
Small three-lamp lighting kit	to XLR
Stands, barn-doors	Output adaptors*
Dichroic blue filters	Sex change barrels, 10, 20 and
Scrims and diffusers	60 db attenuator pads
Mains extension leads and distribution boxes	Batteries for audio mixer and
Good selection of adaptors to match European/	mikes
US supply sockets	
Mobile cell-net telephone	
Hand-held two-way communications radio	

---

* A variety of output adaptors to match the feed sockets, when the audio signal originates from another source. It is advisable to have XLRs, every type of single and double jack and open enders. It is also a good idea to have some leads reversed.

86

THE CAMERA VEHICLE

An essential piece of equipment for the news crew. All items, down to the
smallest, should be clearly marked for easy identification.

Auxiliary equipment (see also list opposite)
Gaffer tape
Tool-kit
Multimeter
Spare fuses
Spare bulbs
Torch
Golf umbrella
Rubber doorstops
Portable TV
Monitor (battery/mains)
Extra BNC-BNC
Cables
Light reflector umbrella
Audio isolating transformer
Short-wave radio
Reporter's notepads
Computer terminal

Wear Sturdy Footwear to Give Your Feet Maximum Protection

Camera common sense
Although sound technical knowledge, 'artistic' and editorial judgement and a hunger for success are accepted as being essential in every ENG camera-operator's make-up, what distinguishes the outstanding from the merely ordinary is often down to a matter of good old-fashioned common sense.

Routine preparations
- Listen to radio news and watch TV. Read the newspapers and keep abreast of current events: the more you already know, the easier your assignment.
- Be prepared to spend some nights away from home at short notice. Always carry an overnight bag with a change of clothes and toiletries.
- Never be without your passport, press identity documents and credit/charge cards.
- Wear substantial shoes. You are likely to be sent to the scene of accidents and disasters where shattered glass and masonry litter the area. Give your feet maximum protection.
- On the road, use your cell-phone to remind those at base to keep you updated on the story line. Where possible they may also be able to provide names of contacts who will be useful on location.
- Never think your story is uninteresting and doomed to the waste bin. This can induce an unprofessional approach. It is not unknown for an unexpected development to transform a routine assignment into a lead story.

Your car
- Have it regularly and professionally maintained.
- Keep it topped up with fuel, especially when driving home at the end of the day. You may be called in the middle of the night, when most service stations are closed.
- Pack your equipment in the most ergonomic and logical way, ensuring camera, recorder, tripod and other essentials are immediately accessible. Having decided the best layout, stick to it, so that if an item goes missing it will be immediately apparent.
- Label everything down to the smallest item, with your own identification mark. You may at times be working alongside many other crews on assignment which demand the use of most of your equipment – two or three sound feeds, radio microphones, mains power units, numerous cables, lights, etc. Under these circumstances equipment can easily go astray and you can be sure the missing item is always the one you need urgently on your next assignment!
- Keep a good set of maps with you. Develop road-craft. Get to know short cuts to avoid time-consuming traffic jams.

Parking
This is a perennial problem for camera crews working in or around urban areas. On arrival at a location, make sure the car is parked so that it is possible to drive off without delay. It is better to park some distance away than risk being boxed in.

PACKING THE CAMERA CAR

Label every item of your equipment and pack it in the car so it is easily accessible. In particular, make sure the camcorder or camera and recorder, tripod, audio mixer and other essential items are immediately to hand. Putting everything in the same place every time will ensure familiarity and speed off the mark. The camera/recorder should always be loaded with a fresh cassette. For the sake of security, cover the equipment with a groundsheet when the vehicle is unattended.

Always Put 30 Seconds of Colour Bars at the Start of Each Tape

Ready for action

Assignments editors expect their crews, whether staff or freelance, to be workmanlike and reliable, so always be ready to start work immediately on arrival at your location.

Equipment

- Keep a full complement of charged batteries.
- Check that the camera has not been switched on in error and that the battery is still fully charged.
- Make sure you have a good supply of fresh tapes.
- Clean the camera lens and viewfinder eyepiece regularly.
- Anticipate lighting conditions, especially where the camera cannot be pre-set. Before leaving for home in the dark, white balance on tungsten: the colour balance will probably be about right if you happen across a story on the journey. Conversely, in the morning daylight, white balance to 5600K before setting out (see page 40).
- Record 30 seconds of colour bars at the start of each tape. The information this provides is invaluable to engineers in the transfer and analysis process.

Climate

Remember that cameras and recorders do not respond well to sudden changes in temperature and humidity. To take a camera from a cool, air-conditioned room into a hot, humid atmosphere creates many problems. The lens and eyepiece will steam up. The recorder will not function. It may take half-an-hour for the whole camcorder to reach the ambient temperature before it is possible to start shooting. So try to store your equipment in corresponding temperature and humidity conditions.

A similar problem occurs when shooting in freezing temperatures and then immediately having to move into a warm building. The only solution to this is to be patient. In these conditions remove the tape from the recorder at once, as condensation may soften the magnetic coating, in turn clogging the heads.

Tape logging

Put yourself in the nightmare position of the picture editor surrounded by a dozen or more tapes shot on a major story, in different locations by four or five crews – none of whom identified their work adequately or even at all.

It makes editing almost impossible. It is therefore essential to have every tape properly marked with the following minimum information on a label on the window side and, if time allows, on the spine as well:

- date
- assignment title
- location
- tape number
- camera operator's name

Labels can often be written before shooting begins. The cassette box should be similarly identified and be accompanied by a detailed log of the coverage, including some indication of the most important shots.

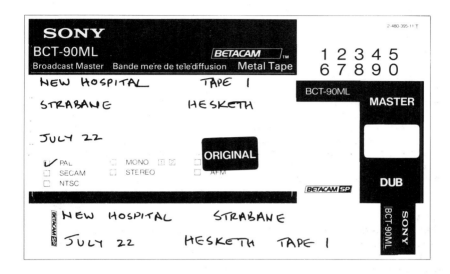

GOOD HOUSEKEEPING

The more you shoot, the more important it is to identify every cassette, otherwise you will inevitably slow down the editing process. The minimum requirement on each label is the title of the story, tape number, location and date, as well as your name. Make sure your writing is legible.

If the Reporter Fails, So Do You

Working with reporters
The most delicate and difficult task facing a camera crew is how to work alongside a reporter to get the most out of a difficult assignment in a hostile environment. Human nature being what it is, what appears on the screen is often likely to be reflected in the way the team behaves towards each other: the greater the mutual liking and professional respect, the better.

The worst . . .
Pairing a lazy reporter with a go-getting camera crew – or vice versa – may be asking for trouble, but sometimes circumstances make it simply impossible to avoid. Camera crews will say the most difficult reporters are beginners who know nothing but mask their inexperience and insecurity with arrogance; bored, unpunctual 'hacks' who have seen it all before and need regularly to be hauled out of bed or bar to start work; the inefficient or disorganized who are incapable of making and carrying out sensible decisions, then sticking to them; the thoughtless who will not offer to help carry equipment no matter how difficult the going; and super-egoists who ignore the advice of experienced colleagues and put their careers before their own and others' safety for the sake of pleasing their superiors.

. . . and the best
At the other end of the scale are the wise, thoughtful professionals who approach every assignment with the same meticulous attention to detail, discuss with their camera crew colleagues every facet of their proposed coverage, welcome practical suggestions and generally treat them as equals not subordinates.

Camera crew attitudes
ENG work is essentially a creative activity, no matter how routine the assignment, and in their turn intelligent reporters expect the camera crews alongside them to contribute positively and enthusiastically.

So remember, as a camera crew on location

- you are part of a team: if the reporter fails, so do you
- your priority is getting the story and getting it back
- be flexible: the next meal break can wait, the story can't
- don't hold back if you have 'editorial' ideas – just offer them tactfully
- don't be offended if a reporter gives 'technical' advice
- don't respond mechanically to suggestions for coverage, particularly if you suspect they are not going to work

And especially

- don't let your work look tired
- seek out the unusual vantage point for a shot which will give your coverage an extra lift
- don't avoid a good location just because it means carrying the equipment an extra distance

WORKING WITH REPORTERS

Good teamwork is essential, especially when crews and reporters find themselves on assignments in the most inhospitable parts of the world. The Gulf War, 1991. (Courtesy of BBC Central Stills).

Don't Let the Reporter Overdo the 'Action'

Pieces to camera

The 'piece to camera' or 'stand-upper' is one of the standard techniques in TV reporting. It is devised to stand by itself or as part of a package, but it has three main purposes: to act as a substitute for scenes difficult or impossible to cover with other pictures; to add emphasis; to prove to the viewer that the reporter is where s/he says s/he is.

The technique

The technique is simple and straightforward. The reporter faces the camera, usually in mid-shot or close-up, and speaks the narrative aloud. Your job is to compose the picture according to style (some news organizations insist the reporter stands in the middle of frame, others prefer to position them to one side). Choose a spot which adds point to the story. Ideally, some activity should be taking place in the background, but it should not be so frenzied as to detract from what the reporter is saying. Make sure there are no children jumping up and down or people aware of and playing to the camera. In framing the shot, take care not to let trees or railings appear to grow from the reporter's body. And beware of offensive graffiti on walls in the background. It is all too easy to miss.

Variations

The classic set-up for the camera is on a tripod two or three inches below the reporter's eyeline as she or he stands full face to the lens. For variety, try moving shots. Walking pieces to camera, using a radio microphone, can be very effective. So can shots on cars or aircraft. But all need careful planning and considerable attention to sound quality. Some reporters covering wars are much given to pieces 'under fire'. Some are phoney: some merely look it. Either way, don't let the reporter overdo it.

Memory problems

Pieces to camera are short – rarely more than a minute (180 words at the average speed of three words to a second). Most reporters can write and memorize their words in a very short time, but some need several takes to get it right, and this can be exasperating for everyone. If there is sufficient time, one way of avoiding this is to get the reporter to learn the piece in two chunks. Record them separately, making sure there is sufficient variety in the two shots so they won't 'jump' when edited together.

A growing alternative to memory is the midget tape-recorder. The reporter records the piece on to tape, places the machine in a pocket, fixes an earpiece into position, and then speaks the words aloud, prompted by the recording. The technique is very effective and seems easy enough, but takes time to accomplish smoothly. The camera-operator's job is to make sure the earpiece and cable are not obviously in shot.

PIECE TO CAMERA

Unless movement is intended, the reporter should keep still at the start and finish of the piece to camera. And make sure no odd facial expressions are made.

Panning or zooming to or from the reporter can be effective if words and pictures match. Rehearse.

As a general rule, keep the reporter's hands out of shot. Nervousness can induce distracting hand movement. (Courtesy of the BBC.)

Dress Should be Appropriate to the Story

Dress sense
Although it is not directly your responsibility, it is important to be aware of any dress code which exists for the reporters in your news organization. In fact, surprisingly few lay down strict rules. Some of those which do, supply 'uniforms' to enforce them. For the majority of reporters using their own wardrobe or making do with a modest clothes allowance, it should be a matter of practicability, good taste and, above all, common sense. No viewer expects to see a male reporter trudging through the jungle wearing a jacket, collar and tie, or a female covering an industrial story in a ball gown. Equally – even in these days of increased informality – the general audience does not deserve to be exposed to an over-casual approach. But some reporters are insensitive, brooking no interference in what they see as a personal matter. They make no concessions to the job, and do not differentiate between what they wear on and off duty.

Use your influence
Allowing for the fact that any opinions about clothing are bound to be subjective, coloured as they are by age and social convention, the most sensible – least controversial – guideline says simply that the reporter should be dressed in a manner appropriate to the story.

As the person behind the camera you can bring quite a lot of influence to bear on what is or is not 'appropriate', and do not hesitate to guide the novice, allowing for the fact that even 'appropriateness' is open to different interpretations: for example, it would seem perfectly appropriate for a reporter in a war zone to be seen wearing military-issue clothing, but whether it is ethically correct may be the subject of fierce debate. On a purely practical level, it would be nonsensical to expect every reporter to carry around a suitcase containing a selection of costumes in the hope that one or other will meet the 'appropriate' requirements, but you should expect your editorial colleagues to follow convention by dressing in a way considered generally acceptable anywhere.

Technical limitations
Some cameras are sensitive to stripes or check patterns which produce an effect known as 'strobing', and it is better to avoid colours which appear to merge the reporter with the background. Bright jewellery and spectacle frames cause 'flare' if they catch the sunlight.

And finally . . .
. . . remember the dress code applies equally to you. Although you are not appearing in front of the camera, you will be judged along with the rest of the team. Don't let them down.

96

DRESS SENSE

Use your influence to ensure inexperienced reporters are dressed suitably for the story. Common sense dictates that the audience will be distracted by the incongruity of a female covering an industrial assignment in evening dress, or a male in the jungle wearing collar and tie. Remember, too, that on location you represent your organization. The casual or scruffy look may be in keeping with the glamorous TV image you may wish to cultivate, but it may also stop you gaining access to some stories.

Position the Interviewee to Look at the Interviewer, Not You

Interviews
Presenters and reporters apart, very few of those who knowingly speak on TV programmes actually make 'speeches'. Most contributors are simply responding to questions put by journalists in the form of 'interviews'. Some of these may be so short as to be barely recognizable or worthy of the term: others are conducted in haste on a doorstep or at leisure in a studio. But what is common to all is that someone has asked a question, and the answer has been captured for TV by an ENG or other camera.

Interviewing as an art-form
Interviewing has developed almost into an art-form in its own right, and those exponents recognized as having a special talent for it often find themselves propelled from the confines of news and current affairs into entertainment or semi-entertainment programmes which have the interview as its basis. One of the best examples is the 'chat show', a format perfect for a star interviewer to display skills honed during a hard journalistic apprenticeship. Guests are invited to submit themselves to interviews which may be soft, mildly probing or deep as agreed, but the interviewer is the star and is as famous or more famous than his guests.

Interview types
Conduct an experiment next time you have the opportunity to watch a full-length TV news programme. Add up the number of people who are seen or heard answering questions, and at the same time note the context, and you will be surprised how many categories of 'interview' you will be able to identify. Include crowded news conferences as well as the question and answer sessions conducted between presenter and reporter in the studio or 'down-the-line' on location.

The role of the camera
The camera's role in every type of interview is to allow the audience the privilege of witnessing what is taking place and – although this may seem contradictory – as unobtrusively as possible. The aim is for every participant who is aware of the camera's presence (remember that interviews are not necessarily between only two people) to be oblivious of it so they respond to each other naturally and spontaneously. The crucial factor in this is the positioning of the camera, and although a studio interview may be conducted in front of two or more, the principle remains the same: the subject of the interview should be framed so that she or he looks and speaks in the direction of the interviewer and not straight at the camera. In this way the oddity of having the interviewee appearing to bypass the questioner and speak straight to the audience is avoided. It is of course not unknown for experienced interviewees to do just the opposite for their own purposes, but that is another matter.

98

INTERVIEWING

Bearing in mind the importance of the background, decide with the reporter in which direction the interviewee will look. Balance the picture with the correct amount of headroom and make sure symmetry is maintained when recording a series of interviews and the reporter's cutaway questions. Your aim is to ensure the subject looks at the interviewer, not directly out of the screen.

Encourage the Participants to Sit Down!

Classic one-to-one interview position
The classic set-up for a single-camera interview between two people is achieved by pointing the lens at the subject over one shoulder of the interviewer. The participants should be virtually opposite each other, the interviewer slightly to one side, but sufficiently close together to allow normal conversation to take place. The interviewee should be framed in medium close-up (head and shoulders) to look across the screen at the questioner.

The aim is to present the interviewee between five and 10 degrees off-centre to the audience to reveal character and reaction. If the two people are placed directly opposite, the interviewee will look straight into the camera, seeming to ignore the questioner: if one is too far to the side, the subject will be in profile, seeming to exclude the viewer. (To create a more 'confrontational' atmosphere the camera is sometimes placed so both interviewer and interviewee are in profile, but this is not a shot to be encouraged in conventional news programmes.)

The artificiality of the TV interview is lessened by these devices, the purpose being to encourage the participants to forget the camera and the audience and to talk directly to each other.

Eyelines and camera height
The other ingredient essential to the credibility of any interview is the eyeline, the direction in which the participants are looking in relation to each other and to the camera, although at this stage no attempt should be made to include both people in shot.

Much depends on camera height and your ability to keep the picture steady, so unless it is totally impossible, always use a tripod, the height of which should be such that the lens is no higher than the interviewee's eyes. Two people talking together face to face will invariably look down during an extended interview, so position the lens just below eyeline level.

Sitting down or standing up?
Some tense interviewees fidget and move about, at worst out of frame. If they can be seated it restricts their movements, but avoid putting them in swivel chairs. When there is more than one interviewee it can be difficult for the reporter to control and equally difficult for the camera-operator to cover. If possible, arrange an order in which the people will speak, but be prepared for a breakdown in that order and for the interviewees to talk among themselves. Sometimes this can make good television but it can also produce a situation which complicates editing.

100

The very tall reporter and
small interviewee

They are too close
together and the camera
angle too steep

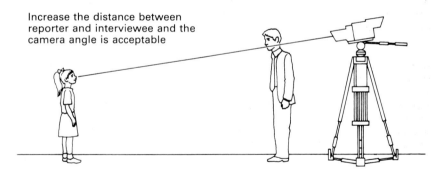

Increase the distance between
reporter and interviewee and the
camera angle is acceptable

DIFFICULT MOMENTS

Dealing with eyeline problems.

The Watchwords are Relevance and Common Sense

Interview backgrounds
The advice is simple enough to give: find the background most appropriate to the interview. But it is rarely as easy as that, because the 'right' background – as with pieces to camera (see page 94) – depends on so many factors, not all of which are under your control. Yet at all times it is essential to keep in mind your main purpose, which is to provide the viewer with pictorial information complementary to what is being said in the interview.

Relevance and common sense
- relevance says locate an interview with a factory manager against the background of activity taking place on the factory floor
- common sense suggests there might be so much movement or noise inside it would be too distracting
- relevance says interview a farmer in his field or barn if the talk is of farming; interview a scientist among the test tubes if the subject is science
- common sense says if the scientist is talking about farming and the farmer about science it might be just as relevant to switch
- common sense suggests, if you can't avoid filming on a flight-path or by a busy roadside, be prepared for interruptions; and make sure the 'quiet' office-located interview remains just that – a ringing telephone can be as disruptive as any jet noise

Putting the subject at ease
For most people, being interviewed for TV is a nerve-racking experience, especially under the bright lights of a studio. Although location interviews may be considered less daunting, particularly when they are taking place on anything resembling 'home ground', the appearance of camera, recorder, microphone and accompanying crew can induce nervousness in the uninitiated.

Don't attempt to turn a subject's inexperience to your advantage: the sole purpose of any interview is to present the viewing audience with fact, opinion, or an opportunity to make up their own minds on matters of importance, and your aim must be to provide an environment in which the interviewee can be at ease and give of their best.

- allow enough time for a dry-run (rehearsal without the camera operating) but not to rehearse an entire interview – it will inevitably spoil spontaneity
- if more than one camera is being used (as in a full studio) explain which is being used for which shot
- tell the interviewee to look at the interviewer, not at you
- if a necktie is undone or a button missing, say so before starting the camera – if it seems necessary, offer a comb

CHOOSING THE RIGHT BACKGROUND

Relevance might be interviewing the factory worker on the factory floor. Common sense suggests it might be too noisy or distracting, so shoot it outside.

Change Shot During the Question, Not the Answer

Interview in progress
The logical first step in a single-camera interview is usually to record a silent two-shot for five or six seconds, to show interviewer and interviewee sharing the same space (there is, of course, nothing to stop you doing this at the end). You will also need an introductory shot of about 10 seconds of the interviewee listening to the reporter, working, or walking into and out of picture.

The opening question
Concentrate on the subject during the interview proper. If you are not under direction, it will be up to you to call out 'running', 'action', or some other predetermined command, as the signal for the interviewer to ask the first question — remembering to leave a few seconds of tape run-up time for the picture editor. Keep the shot steady, and change the picture format only during a question, not an answer. 'News' interviews are short, and shot-changes together with editing later would make the interview seem jumpy. During long interviews, careful shot-changes, especially close-ups, can be extremely telling.

Interviews: one plus two
A single-camera operation is not ideally suited to situations in which the interviewer faces two people at the same time. Composing the shot, balancing the sound and getting the lighting right is difficult enough. On the editorial side it is not unknown for two strong personalities to overwhelm a weak or inexperienced interviewer by starting a conversation between themselves. On other occasions a single dominant interviewee may hog the camera. From time to time, though, you may not be able to avoid double-handers, and so have to make the best of them. The most important thing is to avoid panning the camera from side to side, as if following a tennis ball over the net, as each interviewee answers a question. Even fairly gentle movements soon become difficult to watch.

Position the camera to give a widish medium close-up of both subjects over the interviewer's shoulder. As far as you can, work out a method which will enable you to know in advance who is going to answer. The convention is that the last person mentioned is next to speak, so the simplest way is for the interviewer to preface each question with the interviewee's name: provided that the question is long enough, by the time the answer begins you should have been able to focus on the correct person. Make sure the answer is complete before you think about changing your shot, especially as there's nothing to prevent an interviewee being asked a supplementary or more than one question in succession.

It is easy enough to convert the standard silent two-shot into a three-shot by zooming out to include the whole group: for variety move the camera more to one side. The resulting 'profile' view, used sparingly, can be quite effective.

104

TWO-SHOTS

To zoom out from a close-up of the interviewee to a wide shot which includes the reporter, you will probably have to move the camera back about 3m. Otherwise the reporter may seem disproportionately large in relation to the subject.

When recording a two-shot make sure the interviewee does not talk, is looking at the reporter, and that facial expression matches the interview coverage. Don't have a smiling two-shot with a serious interview: it won't intercut.

A Technique for 'Inserting' the Interviewer

Reverse-angles
The number of electronic cameras used in a TV studio is dependent on the type and complexity of programme being produced. A typical light entertainment show might employ five or six cameras to provide a wide variety of shots, while news or current affairs, with less need for frills, may have use for only three, perhaps four at most. The common factor in both programme types is the link which allows the studio director in the control room to illustrate each passing moment by choosing the picture from the most appropriate camera.

Studio interview set-up
In the case of the light entertainment show, the studio director is able for example to introduce a selection of angles of both performers and audience responses: a director responsible for a studio interview for news is able to weave in shots of the interviewer asking questions or reacting to answers. Three cameras are needed for this exercise (see diagram opposite):

- one camera on the subject
- the second on the interviewer
- the third provides a two-shot

As the camera lens concentrates on each speaker in turn, this makes for pleasant and natural viewing. The shots of the interviewer also offer a useful continuity device when recorded interviews are edited. The alternative is the 'jump' cut which looks both ugly and obvious.

Single-camera set-up
With a single ENG camera on location, the opportunity for variation within a recorded interview is lost, for unless there is a departure from the classic 'over-the-shoulder' set-up, it is not possible to see the faces of interviewer and interviewee in the same shot. Hearing a disembodied voice asking questions probably does not discomfit an audience hearing only 'bite' size answers, but any interview of substantial length is going to appear slightly odd without at least a token glimpse of the reporter.

A beginner might think the way to overcome the problem would be to 'film' each question, followed in turn by each answer. But this is simply not on, as it would mean moving the camera (and possibly lights) every time. The professional's answer is therefore to keep the camera trained throughout the interview on the most important subject – the interviewee – and move it only once, at the end, so the reporter can be shown asking the questions.

These shots are known as reverses, reverse-angles, cut-ins or cutaways, and again the purpose is two-fold: to insert the questioner naturally into the scene where he or she belongs, and to provide material for possible editing points later.

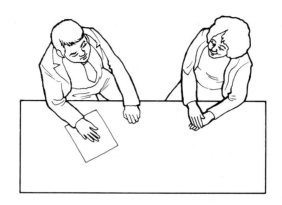

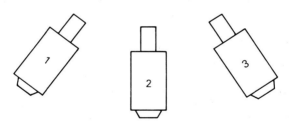

STUDIO INTERVIEW SET-UP

In contrast to single-camera location ENG, three cameras may be used to offer variety during a one-to-one interview in the studio. One camera concentrates on the subject, the second on the interviewer and the third is free to cover a two-shot of both participants.

Take Care Not to Have Both Subjects Facing the Same Way

Reverse-angle technique

All the techniques involved in shooting a reverse-angle of an interview are geared to one outcome – re-creating for the camera the interviewee's eye view of the person asking the questions. On screen, the interviewer should be seen asking the question while looking naturally in the direction of the interviewee – a simple enough effect to achieve with a little practice, but it is surprising how many camera-operators find it difficult, and all manner of mistakes are made, even by those who would consider themselves among the most experienced.

The worst examples appear comic, with interviewer and interviewee seeming to look in the same direction. In others the eyelines fail to match – one is too high, too low or simply slightly misdirected. The outcome is that the reverses are (should be) unusable.

How to do it

Reverses are usually carried out when the subject has already departed, sometimes long afterwards. The interviewer simply repeats for the camera some or all of the questions asked in the interview, referring perhaps to notes or replaying the original to duplicate tone and content as accurately as possible.

For the crew, the simplest method of all is to move the camera and point it at the interviewer from behind the position previously occupied by the interviewee, keeping the lens at the same height as before.

Make sure the background is in character with the scene behind the interviewee. It may be necessary to 'cheat' the position to ensure that the reporter seems to belong in the same environment. Sometimes the only available position is the one used for the subject. If so, be aware of the dangers of exactly the same background: successive shots showing interviewer and interviewee framed against the same landscape or painting will have the audience puzzled or distracted, if not rolling in the aisles.

But the priority is to ensure that the reporter asking the question looks in the opposite direction to the subject. If during the interview the subject was looking five degrees left of frame, the reporter should be positioned to look five degrees right of frame.

Composing the picture

It may seem obvious, but remember also that the shot of the interviewer should match that of the interviewee. Don't let the reporter dwarf the subject, as a big close-up of a reporter asking a question, followed immediately by a wide shot of an interviewee answering it would look distinctly odd. If for some good reason it is not possible to match shots, it is more acceptable to have the interviewee appear slightly larger.

108

(1)

(2)

(3)

REVERSE-ANGLES

On-location interviews for news are usually conducted with a single camera.
Reverse-angle shots of the reporter asking questions are carried out afterwards,
often inserted during editing as a device for bridging sections of interview. After
the interview (1) move the camera or the reporter and record the reverses making
sure the eyeline is a faithful reproduction of the original position (2). The edited
version will then have reporter and interviewee look towards each other (3) and
not in the same direction.

Help the Reporter Re-create the Interview Mood

'Noddies' and 'listening shots'
Once the camera has been set up correctly, the next step is to ensure the technique seems natural. Interviewers are not actors, and without the presence of the interviewee at the end of what might have been a highly charged occasion, they may come across as unconvincing, unsure exactly where to look, what tone of voice to use, and (perhaps) forgetful of the questions they have only just asked.

Your job, behind the camera, is to help re-create the mood. If it helps to make the interviewer's eyeline accurate, put someone in the interviewee's place. Experienced interviewers usually carry their own miniature tape-recorders which they activate during interviews; others jot their questions down in notebooks or on clipboards. On the rare occasion this does not happen, play back the interview so that tone and content can be judged correctly. Encourage the interviewer to get them right.

The ethics of reverses
Although the cutaway question is a well-established and effective technique, an increasing number of TV professionals express unease about using a device which apparently encourages falsification of events, and some news organizations ban it as a result. Others allow the insertion of reverses, but ban the 'noddy', a variation which gives the impression the reporter understands the answers. The danger here is that interviewers seen nodding their heads might be thought to be in agreement with what is being said – innocuous enough most of the time, perhaps, but controversial in some circumstances. You are in the best position to advise. A 'steady listening shot' might be regarded as a more acceptable alternative, but few reporters are able to carry this off with much conviction, instead gazing woodenly in the general direction of the interviewee.

Alternatives to reverses
Although reverse-angles and noddy shots are falling into disrepute, their purpose remains proper enough: to provide a continuity bridge between sections of interviews instead of the inelegant 'jump' which appears on screen at every edit. But if editorial principle does rule them out, and assuming jump-cuts are unacceptable, what are the alternatives?

- Plan coverage of the interview to allow composition to be altered during questions: in this way, edits may appear more as definite shot-changes and less as the near-subliminal 'twitches' apparent from cuts made into material shot at the same lens focal length.
- Mix between edited sections. This needs the post-production collaboration of the picture editor, and 'tight' edits may not always lend themselves to the technique. However, a mix makes the audience aware an edit has taken place, but it does so in a way which does not jar the senses.

110

'STEADY LISTENING SHOTS'

An alternative editing device to the reverse-angle of the reporter asking a question is the 'steady listening shot'. Make it long enough (minimum 3 seconds) to register. It should give the impression that the reporter understands the answers but not that she or he agrees with what is being said, as this could be controversial in some circumstances.

Difficulties on the Doorstep

Interview problems

Although you will find a large number of interview assignments simple and straightforward, with the interviewees collaborating willingly if not with much enthusiasm, the nature of news means there are bound to be occasions when the opposite is the case. Ethical considerations are discussed elsewhere (see page 174), so what we are considering here are the more obvious problems associated with interview situations in which you have little or no opportunity to choose the time or location, set up the camera properly or exercise any real control over what is happening.

'Door-steppers'

The term 'door-stepper' was coined to describe the interview which sometimes takes place literally on the doorstep, as reporters and camera crews wait to talk to the newsworthy. It is a common enough sight at modern news events. A scrum of media people jostles for position, recorders and microphones thrust forward to catch any words thrown in their direction. As it happens, most door-steppers are barely worthy of the description 'interview' as they tend to consist of nothing more enlightening than a grudging sentence or two or an unambiguous 'no comment'.

But sometimes door-steppers do produce something worth while, and as a cameraman on such an assignment your task is to ensure that whatever is said is captured for the audience, so you cannot afford to be separated from your recordist, if you have one. The important thing to remember is that as soon as the reporter is on the move, you must start the tape and keep it running: you do not want to be caught cold.

In these circumstances if your own reporter is unsuccessful, someone else in the crowd may not have been, and as 'copyright' cannot be claimed over the recording of current events (see page 168), in most cases it will be legitimate to use anything which comes out of the scuffle.

'Snatched' interviews

A 'snatched' interview suggests less of a scrum than the door-stepper, to which it is probably first cousin. A typical example is the unexpected 'conversation' attempted by the reporter as the subject gets into a car. Here again, it is essential to have the camera focused and running, with microphone at the ready. Otherwise by the time you are up to speed, the 'interview' may be over.

DOORSTEP INTERVIEWS

A phenomenon of modern news-coverage. Camera crews and reporters waiting 'on the doorstep' for the chance of an interview. (Courtesy of Sussex Police)

Getting it Back – 1

If the introduction of ENG in the mid-seventies revolutionized the philosophy and practice of news-gathering, without the parallel development of global communications systems the revolution would have been stillborn. For if no means had been found of delivering the electronic signals speedily across continents, the whole process would have been locked into a time-warp along with the 16mm newsfilm images which sometimes took days from location to reach the point of transmission.

Communications satellites
Satellites were born out of the need for fast and effective communication for military and space exploration purposes. Now they circle the earth, picking up signals from ground stations and then redirecting them to others. A global system for telecommunications began to take shape in the sixties with the foundation of the International Telecommunications Satellite Organisation (Intelsat). Well over 100 countries are now members. From their position 22 300 miles (36 000km) above the Pacific, Atlantic and Indian ocean regions, the satellites appear stationary, giving complete and continuous coverage across the globe. Thousands of ground stations exist to send and receive telephone, fax, data, radio and TV communications from all over the world.

DBS
The rapid development of satellites now allows for precise transmission to individual homes by way of tiny dish aerials (hence Direct Broadcasting by Satellite or Direct-to-Home Broadcasting) and the establishment of alternative broadcast systems. The British-based 'Sky News' and Ted Turner's 'Cable News Network' (CNN) are among the examples of organizations which have made use of the technology to challenge the previous invincibility of the conventional, terrestrial news broadcasters. Other specialist news-related services have also made their mark, although the huge expense involved has already led to casualties among the pioneers, and it may be well into the next century before the dust settles and all the players become established.

Satellite news-gathering
Now, instead of having to feed signals to the satellite along a 'gateway' to a commercial 'uplink', some of the wealthier news organizations have invested in their own miniature ground stations which are portable enough to be flown or driven to important assignment locations at home or abroad. This 'satellite news-gathering' made an extremely effective contribution to the coverage of the 1991 Gulf War, allowing material to be sent direct to the orbiting satellites for onward transmission.

THE SPEED OF COMMUNICATIONS

Man-made communications satellites orbiting the earth 36 000km above the equator have enabled sound and picture signals to reach TV stations almost instantaneously from virtually anywhere in the world. Tiny dish aerials have become familiar sights on rooftops everywhere with the growth in popularity of direct-to-home systems offering a range of international services, including all-news channels. The global system began to revolutionize the coverage of foreign news in the early sixties, but developments for television and other forms of telecommunication are barely out of their infancy.

Ground Stations are Small Enough to be Taken as Excess Baggage

Satellites at war

The Gulf War, which began with the invasion of Kuwait by Iraqi forces in August 1990, has since become accepted as opening a new phase in the development of foreign news coverage – the launching pad for television satellite feeds direct from an operational zone. As the failure of diplomacy hardened into a shooting war at the beginning of 1991, every leading news organization had its own or access to satellite earth terminals in Iraq, Saudi Arabia, Jordan, Israel and the desert battlefronts, to provide immediate, high-quality pictures and sound of the conflict direct into homes across the world.

Flight cases support the dish

This advance was made possible by the development of new, compact earth terminals. All the components fit snugly into specially designed flight cases, giving previously unobtainable levels of protection against shock, vibration and sudden changes in environment. The cases conform to the standards of the International Air Transport Association (IATA) which allows them to be shipped as excess baggage. One of the most effective systems in the Gulf was provided by the Advent company's Mantis 1500/1900 antenna, which was capable of operating with most of the geostationary satellites in use or planned. The flight cases lock together to form a substantial structure to support the reflector (dish) mount and the electronic units. The reflector is made up of eight segments.

Site selection

Careful site selection is important, as there must be a clear line of sight to the designated satellite. The signal can be weakened by proximity to metal structures, trees and shrubs with a high water content, and strong winds can shift the antenna's critical alignment to the satellite.

Safety is an important feature of the unit, and the operator and equipment are protected from the entry of water into the wave guides. Compass and azimuth bearings are supplied to help in locating the satellite, which has its own transmitting beacon identification for precise alignment. A colour monitor, displaying the satellite's transmissions, will help.

The unit also has a videotape machine with a built-in time base corrector. Transmissions from the terminal can be made only with permission of, and at the times agreed by, the local telecommunications authority or satellite operator.

Realistically, only trained engineers are able to operate this specialized equipment efficiently, and the engineer is a valued member of a news team who may be operating thousands of miles from home base.

SATELLITE NEWS-GATHERING

Portable satellite news-gathering systems allowed international coverage of events in the 1991 desert war between Iraq and a United Nations coalition to be broadcast live or with very little delay. (Courtesy of Advent Communications.).

Getting it Back – 2

Never delay and risk missing your deadline

In today's fiercely competitive world, any news organization which is regularly seen failing to get its stories on the air at approximately the same time as – or preferably ahead of – its rivals is sure to lose credibility with the audience. As a member of a camera crew you must regard yourself as part of a bigger team, and you will contribute to its success by following the essential rule of despatch: never delay and miss your deadline or bulletin time as a result. Of course there are times when leaving the location means risking missing the main or essential element of a story. This demands sound journalistic judgement, especially when it is impossible to predict the timing of events.

Planning the cut-off point

As a regular part of your routine you should plan in advance the point at which you need to break off your coverage and the method you intend to use to ensure it reaches its destination. Your calculation should include not only the time it may take to get there, but also an allowance for the editing process, bearing in mind the complexity and duration of what you have shot. Having made your decision, do not be tempted to wait 'just another five minutes'.

There are then several ways of ensuring your material gets to its destination.

Driving it home

The simplest option is to collect the cassettes of camera rushes you have shot and take them back at the end of the assignment. Use your own transport, but be sure your vehicle is parked for a quick getaway. Know your area – the main and alternative routes – and have a good set of maps.

Motorcycle couriers

Some of the more affluent news organizations employ motorcycle despatch riders to allow the camera team to stay on the story by ferrying material from location back to base. Most are very thoughtful, fuelling a team on stake-out with coffee and sandwiches!

Microwave links

This is usually another vehicle, staffed by a qualified engineer. It is equipped with replay machines and a facility to transmit the signal, given good conditions, up to about 80 miles (130km). Sometimes a despatch rider will be used to take the material from the crew on location to the links vehicle.

'Loco points'

Television networks in big cities provide cable, video and sound links called 'loco points' from which material can be fed back to their switching centres. These are strategically placed close to the centres of government, industry and commerce.

(1)

(2)

MICROWAVES

Editing and replay equipment installed in microwave links vehicles can speed ENG sound and pictures on their way from location to home base. In good conditions signals can be transmitted up to about 130km. ((1) Courtesy of the Sussex Police, (2) Courtesy of the BBC.)

Getting it Back – 3

Over-shooting wastes valuable satellite time
It will come as a shock to find that the process of getting your raw material back to base from a foreign assignment presents more problems than you faced while undertaking the coverage itself. This is especially true of stories to be sent back before you move on to cover another item, or for the stories you have shot to be returned in 'instalments'.

Flying with the 'bird'
As we have seen, the establishment of communications satellite systems has revolutionized foreign reporting to the extent of making same-day coverage possible from almost anywhere in the world. For you, the process of 'birding' (named after Early Bird, the first satellite launched by Intelsat, page 114) is a matter of planning to ensure circuits are arranged for times convenient to you and the programme deadlines you aim to meet. Bookings can be arranged at the receiving end, usually by those responsible for foreign news-gathering. Circuits are expensive and cancellation charges high, so arrive at the feed point in good time. It also follows that you should be disciplined in the shooting of your story, so when sending unedited material valuable transmitting time is not wasted. This applies equally when you take your material direct to a satellite station or your own organization's mobile ground station.

Shipping by air
If your material is not urgent, it may well be sensible to send it home as air cargo. Except in dire circumstances you would be advised to avoid transhipment in favour of a direct flight, even if it is scheduled to arrive a little later. Airports around the world are now quite familiar with the process, but find out in advance the time at which your material has to arrive at cargo depots so the necessary formalities can be completed before your chosen flight. You will need to ask for a form of receipt known as an air waybill. Advise your base of the waybill and flight numbers and the estimated arrival time of the aircraft. The shipping agent will do the rest. Not that it is always so simple.

Dealing with customs officials
On some occasions you will have to contend with censorship and the bureaucracy of customs offcials. Tapes and scripts may need to be submitted to and passed by a censor, who will probably operate from a government or state press bureau. This time-consuming process is usually compounded by the need for customs clearance, as officials will not normally allow export without a sheaf of export papers and a sight of the censor's clearance documents. The problem is often exacerbated by the need to complete paperwork written in a foreign language. In these circumstances try to recruit a good shipping agent who is aware of any special local conditions and can help smooth your path.

Do not insert carbon. Write with firm pressure in block capitals on a hard surface.

Fix the lines here

236- 5017616 2

Shipper's Name and Address	Shipper's Account Number

Not negotiable

Express Air Waybill

PRIORITY *EXPRESS*

Issued by
British Midland Airways Limited
Donington Hall, Castle Donington, Derby DE7 2SB

Consignee's Name and Address	Consignee's Phone Number

IMPORTANT NOTICE

If the carriage involves an ultimate destination or stop in a country other than the country of departure, the Warsaw Convention may be applicable and the Convention governs and in most cases limits the liability of carriers in respect of loss or damage to the cargo - see also conditions overleaf.

No. of Packages	Actual Gross Weight Kilos	Description of Goods

Issuing Carrier's Agent Name and City	Account No.

General Sales Agent
INTERNATIONAL CARGO MARKETING LTD.
Donington Hall, Castle Donington,
Derby, DE7 2SB. England.

Weight Charge	Cartage	Other Charges	Total

Airport of Departure (Addr. of first Carrier) and Requested Routing

to	By First Carrier	to	by	to	by	Currency	CHGS Code	Prepaid	Declared Value for Carriage	Declared Value for Customs

Airport of Destination	Flight /Date	For Carrier Use only/ Flight/Date	Amount of Insurance	INSURANCE - If Carrier offers insurance, and such insuranc is requested in accordance with conditions on reverse hereof, indicate amount to be insured in figures in box marked 'amount of insurance'

Handling Information

(For USA only) These commodities licensed by U.S. for ultimate destination .... Diversion contrary to U.S. law is prohibited

Shipper certifies that the particulars on the face hereof are correct that in so far as no part of the consignment contains live animals, plants or hazardous and dangerous goods within the meaning of the current Dangerous Goods Regulations

Signature of Shipper or his Agent

Executed on   (Date)   at   (Place)   Signature of Issuing Carrier or its Agent

Agent

AIR WAYBILL

Completion of the correct documentation is essential if material sent by air cargo is to reach its destination without delay. Many news organizations employ shipping agents to trace and collect incoming tapes, clear them through customs, pay any duty, and deliver them (Waybill reproduced courtesy of British Midland). The ATA Carnet System (see page 123) is used for the movement of equipment.

The Most Willing Passenger May Get 'Cold Feet'

Hand-carrying

Wars, coup d'détats and various other forms of civil unrest have an almost inevitable tendency to make governments extremely nervous about the image they present overseas, and one of their first reactions is to close the normal channels of media communication. Telephone links are cut, TV and radio transmitters surrounded by armed guards and satellite ground stations mysteriously put out of action. All that are left operational are perhaps a few airline services.

The 'pigeon'

To circumvent these difficulties, a carefully selected passenger, known in the business as a 'pigeon', may be approached at the airport and persuaded to carry as part of their personal luggage the precious video material you have shot. This works often enough because passengers are flattered to be entrusted with such a simple task which usually ends up in a hand-over meeting at an airport or railway station. Some pigeons may even be persuaded to make delivery right to the door of your TV station, but there are also many occasions when 'office representative' and pigeon manage to miss each other in the crowd, there is confusion over the rendezvous or the package incredibly is mislaid or left on the aircraft.

The risk of 'cold feet'

At other times, mindful of bomb scares and security baggage checks, the most willing traveller may get 'cold feet' at the last moment and just dump your precious cargo in a waste-bin or even hand it to the security people. This could spell trouble for you. So if possible give it to someone whom you know is thoroughly reliable, perhaps a member of the aircrew. A word of warning: there is of course an ever-present element of risk when trying to bypass officials channels. If caught, you may well end up in prison, where you quickly learn how many local laws you have broken.

Collaborating with the competition

In some circumstances it may pay handsome dividends to send a member of your own camera team on the flight, perhaps carrying material shot by other TV crews as well as yours. Despite the generally cut-throat nature of the business, this strictly unofficial arrangement between rivals is often worth considering, on the basis that your turn to rely on them will surely come at some future time.

. . . and other ways

Finally, do not forget the railways. Most systems offer reliable cargo-handling facilities for small parcels or packets, some guaranteeing arrival within specified periods. Above all, be encouraged by the determination of other camera crews to get their material home from the hottest of hot-spots.

EUROPEAN COMMUNITY

2 7

Statistical copy — Country of dispatch/export
Statistical copy — Country of destination

2 Consignee/Exporter   No

8 Consignee   No

14 Declarant/Representative   No

18 Identity and nationality of means of transport at departure/on arrival   19 Ctr.

21 Identity and nationality of active means of transport crossing the border

25 Mode of transport at the border | 26 Inland mode of transport | 27 Place of loading/unloading

2 7   29 Office of exit/entry   30 Location of goods

1 DECLARATION   A OFFICE OF DISPATCH/EXPORT/DESTINATION

3 Forms | 4 Loading lists

5 Items | 6 Total packages | 7 Reference number

9 Person responsible for financial settlement   No

10 Cty. lst. dest./last consig. | 11 Trad./Prod. country | 12 Value details | 13 CAP

15 Country of dispatch/export | 15 C. disp./exp. Code | 17 Country destin. Code

16 Country of origin | 17 Country of destination

20 Delivery terms

22 Currency and total amount invoiced | 23 Exchange rate | 24 Nature of transaction

28 Financial and banking data

31 Packages and description of goods   Marks and numbers — Container No(s) — Number and kind   32 Item No   33 Commodity Code

34 Country origin Code | 35 Gross mass (kg) | 36 Preference

37 PROCEDURE | 38 Net mass (kg) | 39 Quota

40 Summary declaration/Previous document

41 Supplementary units | 42 Item price | 43 VM Code

44 Additional information/Documents produced/Certificates and authorisations   A.I. Code | 45 Adjustment

46 Statistical value

47 Calculation of taxes   Type | Tax base | Rate | Amount | MP   48 Deferred payment | 49 Identification of warehouse

B ACCOUNTING DETAILS

Total:

50 Principal   No   Signature   C OFFICE OF DEPARTURE

51 Intended offices of transit (and country)   represented by   Place and date:

52 Guarantee not valid for   Code | 53 Office of destination (and country)

D/J CONTROL BY OFFICE OF DEPARTURE/DESTINATION   Stamp   54 Place and date:
Result:
Seals affixed: Number: Signature and name of declarant/representative
Identity:
Time limit (date):
Signature:

C88A   Printed in the UK for HMSO 8055019 9/87 W.B.F. F5887 (SEPT. 1987) 910/55 485944

THE 'PASSPORT FOR GOODS'

Taking equipment abroad and bringing it back after an assignment is almost impossible without proper planning and documentation. The ATA Carnet, known popularly as the 'Passport for Goods', is presented to Customs authorities at each exit, entry and transit point of an international journey. The document includes a detailed description of the goods to be despatched, with an undertaking to pay the duty and tax liabilities if they are not returned. The undertaking consists of bank guarantees or a lodged security of a value comparable with that of the equipment. Although the need for documentation is easing within the EC, crews in Europe could be assigned onwards to countries where the Carnet is still demanded. It is also useful evidence if any of your equipment is lost or stolen. (Customs and Excise Form C88A is Crown Copyright and is reproduced with the permission of the Controller of Her Majesty's Stationery Office.)

Wasting Tape Wastes Time in the Editing Suite

Thinking of the picture editor
It is often said that one of the surest ways of understanding the craft of film-making is to learn editing. A spell in the editing suite teaches continuity and generally what works – and what doesn't – in visual terms. In news, even though the scope is more limited, camera-operators can in effect become their own editors if they shoot with the next link of the production chain in mind.

Shooting for the edit suite
Whatever the subject, what most news programmes want from their teams in the field is good raw material which can easily be assembled in sufficient time to meet the next deadline. What they do not want is to be overwhelmed and have to plough through an hour's worth of tape to service a three- or four-minute routine item.

The secret lies in thorough planning and execution: even if you are working with experienced producers or editors with their own strong ideas about the coverage, the duration, composition and quality of each shot and sequence is likely to be under your control. Retakes for editorial or external reasons are at times unavoidable, but try to keep them to a minimum. Avoid retakes just 'for safety': better still, if you are able to rehearse each shot without running tape, so much the better. Of course in most hard-news contexts the accent is on anticipation and quick reactions, and the idea of more than rudimentary planning or rehearsal is unthinkable.

Editing in camera
In some circumstances it is possible to put together a complete item using a technique called 'editing in camera' (see opposite page). This requires particularly careful planning and a prepared script, so is limited probably only to fairly simple stories. Shooting is undertaken sequentially, in prearranged order, each shot timed to cover the amount of commentary which is recorded simultaneously. A piece to camera can be included without much difficulty.

Summing up
So the basics can be summed up as follows:

- Don't shoot unnecessarily: the more tape you use, the longer it will take to view. As a rough rule of thumb, aim for a 2 : 1 ratio, i.e. two minutes of raw 'rushes' for every one minute used.
- Shoot in sequences: try to imagine how the finished version is going to appear on the screen.
- Spend time in the editing suite while your item is being assembled. Comments from the picture editor will usually be instructive (if at times embarrassing).

VIDEO	DURATION	AUDIO

1. PAN OVER VALLEY

8 sec. — The residents living around this pleasant little valley could face an invasion from thousands of football fans every year if local authority planners agree.

2. MID-SHOT REPORTER PIECE TO CAMERA

20 sec. — Tomorrow the full Council meets to decide whether to give outline permission to Rovers Football Club, who want to build a new stadium less than a mile away. There would be seats for twelve thousand people and space to park three thousand cars, and the stadium would be ready for occupation in time for the start of next season.

3. ZOOM PAST REPORTER TO MOTORWAY TRAFFIC

13 sec. — What makes this site particularly attractive is its access to the motorway, good public transport, and its nearness to the east end of the town where the club has had its ground for the past ninety-three years.

4. CLOSE-UP NOTICE BOARD WITH FIXTURE LIST

5 sec. — Paradoxically, Rovers have traditionally attracted strong support from among the people here,

5. CLOSE-UP PROTEST POSTER

4 sec. — but tonight protesting residents intend to plan their own campaign at a

6. ZOOM OUT TO GV VILLAGE HALL

14 sec. — special meeting. Because although they know the club has to find a new home or spend millions to meet safety requirements at their current ground, they say the prospect of having Rovers on their doorstep is too high a price to pay.

EDITING IN CAMERA

This is a useful device if editing is not available or very limited. The essential requirement is to keep things simple, shoot in sequence, and rehearse to ensure commentary does not overlap the picture. In this example, a news story lasting just over 1 minute is constructed from six shots, five with the reporter's voice-over recorded simultaneously. The other is a piece to camera.

Unlike Film, Tape is Never 'Cut'

Basic editing methods
There is not a lot to beat the satisfaction of seeing the raw material fresh from the camera spring to life in front of you at the hands of an expert picture editor in the semi-darkness of an editing suite. Editing enhances story-telling, whether it is a simple, 30-second newsbrief about traffic hold-ups or a multi-faceted item about economic matters.

The end of uncertainty
In the days of newsfilm it was at this stage that even the most experienced cameramen suffered pangs of uncertainty, because until the film was processed she or he could never be quite sure whether they had actually captured the images they had seen in the viewfinder, and whether the light exposure they had measured so carefully was accurate. But that uncertainty has gone, because the essence of ENG is that if necessary every shot can be reviewed on-site and repeated if there is the slightest doubt.

Tape editing
The other most significant difference is that videotape material – unlike film – is never physically cut. Instead, cassettes containing the camera rushes are inserted in one machine and the selected shots played across to a second in the correct sequence, and rerecorded one-by-one until a whole item is compiled electronically. If any shot is too short, too long or does not fit for some other reason, the whole process can be repeated without harming the original material or degrading its quality. Selection is made easier by time-coding at the time of shooting, which allows the time of day to be superimposed on the bottom of the picture. This does not, of course, show up when the item is broadcast.

The digital revolution
The present technique, though refined and improved, has been in use since tape superseded film during the mid nineteen-seventies. The next big advance is in 'digital' editing, in which no physical assembly of pictures takes place at all. The editor merely selects sequential 'in' and 'out' points and feeds them into a computerized editing machine which memorizes the co-ordinates and 'joins' the shots into the correct order. Should the editor wish to re-edit, she or he simply makes another selection. The whole process is astonishingly swift and accurate.

The significance of this development should not be lost on camera people or those who class themselves as 'journalists'. Such is the simplicity of the equipment, any member of a production team should be able to operate it effectively with the minimum of instruction. The introduction of digital editing techniques has already begun, and there are confident predictions that they will have largely superseded present methods by the turn of the century.

ENG EDITING

Electronic editing. Unlike film, videotape is never physically cut during the editing process. Instead, sequences are built up by re-recording shots from one videocassette to another. Developments include computerized digital editing equipment and video editing on laptop computers. For reporters in the field there is a Hi8 edit pack built into a single unit about the same size as a home VCR.

A Way to Reduce Picture Instability

Time-base correction
Film sprocket-holes, along with well-engineered camera and projector mechanisms, provide stable moving pictures for celluloid: the equivalent of the sprocket-hole in recorded videotape is the 'sync pulse'. The sync generator feeds precise, stable signals, along with the camera video information, to the recording tape. But the mechanisms which transport videotape are highly intricate and inherently subject to instability.

Jitter, jump and frame bar roll
Despite the rapid advancement of the technology, it has so far been impossible to design a videotape recorder which records at an exactly constant speed. The corollary of that is the impossibility of replaying at precisely the same speed at which the tape was recorded. The video waveform information, exact to one nanosecond (one thousand-millionth of a second), is distorted during replay, creating errors which show up on the picture as jitter, jump and frame bar roll.

These 'time-base' errors can also result from marked temperature change, humidity and recorder movement. Gyroscopic time-base errors are created by rapid and constant movement; for example, a quick pan of the camcorder will almost certainly introduce an error.

The effect of humidity
A tape shot in a hot, humid atmosphere will expand. Return it to the cool of a picture-editing suite and it will contract, introducing yet another time-base error. These errors create real problems for the editor when integrating videotape into the precise sync generator-controlled production process, making it impossible to use fade, dissolve or wipe techniques.

Cleaning up the syncs
The diagram opposite shows how the video lines and horizontal sync pulses can be degraded. (An original recording is considered 'first generation', with subsequent copies a generation removed from the tape from which they were made.) The problem is solved by the Time-Base Corrector. The unstable video signals and degraded sync pulses are fed into the TBC's analogue-to-digital converter and proc amp (Colour Video Processing Amplifier). The proc amp strips away the degraded sync pulses and replaces them with its own self-generated new clean syncs. The revitalized signals, when converted from digital back to the original analogue form, will now interface with the system without a problem.

The new generation of portable videotape recorders now have built in time-based correctors. The signals from other non-synchronous video sources – for example, remote cameras or stations generating their own syncs – are fed into a frame-store and synchronized and processed in order to lock into the network operation.

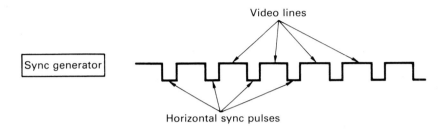

Video lines

Sync generator

Horizontal sync pulses

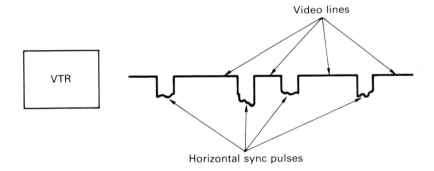

Video lines

VTR

Horizontal sync pulses

TIME-BASED CORRECTION

Regular precise stable pulses produced by the sync pulse generator (1). The same sync pulses now distorted on replay because the VTR cannot precisely match the recording speed (2). The time-base corrector strips away these distorted pulses to replace them with its own self-generated new clean syncs.

Keep Safe and Warm when Filming from Helicopters

Aerial coverage

Aerial shooting offers a dramatic alternative angle to many news stories, especially if reserved for only rare occasions.

Shooting from helicopters

Some networks and leading TV news organizations have their own helicopters, complete with camera mounting and stabilizing system, microwave link equipment, video recorder and a powerful light for night shooting. The installation has to be approved by the Civil Aviation Authority in addition to normal aircraft certification.

Although expensive to buy and maintain, the main advantage of the company-owned helicopter is the speed at which it can be in operation. The camera can be fitted quickly, the camera-operator equipped with safety harness and the aircraft airborne within minutes. The on-board microwave equipment is capable of transmitting audio-video signals over a distance up to 50 miles (80km) into programmes. It can also serve as a mid-point radiofrequency (RF) link, providing engineering and operational communications between the pilot, camera-operator, base engineers and editors. Where 'disaster' stories are involved, the high-intensity searchlight could be a useful aid to emergency services on the ground, enabling the pilot to overfly an area which would otherwise be restricted.

For those without the luxury of company-owned aircraft, arranging aerial coverage is in principle not unlike arranging the hire of any other specialist equipment. Only a limited number of experienced operators are likely to exist, so a routine procedure is worth establishing. If you are dealing with an unfamiliar company, make sure they thoroughly understand and can meet your requirements. Helicopters have flight operational limits – for example, a single-engined machine is not allowed to overfly populated areas, the sea, or undertake night flights.

Covering the story

By the time you reach the helipad the company should have filed the flight plan with the authorities and removed the helicopter door, if it is not of the sliding variety. Shoot from the open hatch, sitting on the floor. But be sure to be properly clothed, as an open helicopter can be very cold, especially in the winter. Wear a full safety-harness, have a safety strap secured to the camera and have headphones with talk-back communication to the pilot. The body will absorb much of the aircraft vibration, but it will be difficult to use a long focal length lens.

The experienced 'photo' pilot will make the task easy, flying or hovering at the correct height and in the right relationship to the sun. Keep the pilot informed of your progress and, if necessary, ask for changes in height or approach. Be aware that the pilot will also have operational limitations.

(1)

(2)

(3)

AERIAL COVERAGE

Helicopters are ideal for certain types of news coverage. Shooting is through the open door, with the camera-operator strapped into a full safety-harness. For night coverage some specially-equipped helicopters have a powerful lamp which can be remotely controlled from inside the cabin. The mounted camera is dockable, the 'back end' fed to a separate recorder. Fixed wing aircraft are to be avoided. They are too fast and lack manoeuvrability, but if there is no alternative it may be possible to remove a window or door and to ask the pilot to fly on a steady course further from the scene to facilitate sustained shots. ((1) Courtesy of Flying Pictures; (2), (3) Courtesy of ITN.)

Be Sparing with Artificial Light at Night

Night shooting
Any news crew involved on routine assignments will sooner or later find themselves shooting external scenes at night. And daunting though this might seem at first, the confidence born of practice and good technique will overcome most of the obvious problems.

Avoiding 'smear'
The first step is to check the viewfinder display if Low Light is indicated. Switch on 9db or 18db to increase the video level, but take care and try to eliminate the vertical 'smear' which affects some cameras. This smear is caused by pinpoints of specular or bright light against a dark background, resulting in excessive overloading of the CCD and the subsequent leaking of the charge into the shift registers. The 'comet tail' trailing from a moving light source, caused by image retention in some tubes and circuitry, can often be reduced by placing the tripod carefully to limit the angle through which the lights appear to move on the screen.

Interviewing at night
Be sparing with the artificial light when shooting an interview or reporter piece to camera against a typical night background. With the iris wide open, use just enough light to expose the face correctly. This should allow the maximum of background detail to be seen. In general, you would be well advised not to use the auto-iris mode when night shooting. Vehicle headlights moving head-on and then out of frame will simultaneously affect the exposure if the iris is fully open.

Dawn and Dusk
These provide some of the finest conditions for the experienced, sensitive operator, because it is possible to create beautifully atmospheric pictures. For the newcomer they offer the perfect opportunity to experiment.

At first light, try shooting without the 5600K filter to enhance the ethereal quality of the scene. The camera should be white-balanced to 3400K or use the pre-set facility without a filter. At this time of day it is particularly important to judge just the correct moment to use the 5600K filter before the blue content becomes unacceptable. The converse applies when shooting at dusk.

Specialist night equipment
Ultrasensitive cameras such as the Ikegami HL 87M offer exceptional performance, allowing scenes to be shot in light barely discernible to the human eye. This is the ideal equipment for extended night coverage of animal movements, etc. (The camera can also be used to shoot in very bright sunlight.) Mini Image Intensifiers, with integral battery-operated power supply, can be fitted between camera body and lens. The intensifier is about 150mm (6 in) long and can produce high-quality black and white pictures at extremely low light levels.

NIGHT SHOOTING

Be sparing with artificial light when shooting an interview or reporter piece to camera against a typical night background. On-camera lighting can be effective, but with the iris wide open use just enough light to expose the face correctly. (Courtesy of PAG.)

Finding the Story is Simpler than Finding a Camera Position

Special occasion coverage

Only in camera crews' dreams does a world exist in which access to the scene of any important national or international event remains unlimited and unfettered. Reality suggests that an efficient system needs to be established wherever the demand for media attention is great, and where the threat of disruption from outside — ranging from mischief-making protest demonstrations to serious terrorist activity — is thought to be a possibility. If by now it is clear that a considerable amount of what appears on the TV screen does so as the result of careful planning and preparation, then it applies to a greater degree to what might be called 'special occasion' coverage, where getting the story is a minor matter compared with overcoming the bureaucracy associated with getting to a position from which you can actually operate the camera.

Press officers

Meeting the legitimate requirements of TV, radio, newspapers and magazines is a logistical nightmare for those given the task. The sheer growth in numbers is in itself fairly awesome: from the 550 accredited correspondents covering the D-day landings of 1944 to about 3500 at the Group of Seven economic summit in London in the summer of 1991 and 5700 at the opening of the Middle East peace conference in Madrid later the same year. Arrangements have to be made to accommodate and feed several thousand impatient, competitive professionals; to make sure they get to wherever the action is — whatever it is — at the right time, and can then communicate what they have seen and heard to their home base. Press or public relations officers, information officers and 'minders' often deserve the criticisms they receive for being obstructive, unhelpful or inefficient, but just as often they deserve praise for smoothing the way towards coverage.

Accreditation

Accreditation — 'official' recognition — may last indefinitely or only as long as the event being covered. For example, journalists accredited to the White House to cover American presidential activities are listed on a computer and as a result are allowed into the regular briefings with a minimum of delay. Foreign correspondents may be accredited to government ministries, thus ensuring them ongoing official co-operation and access to documents denied to others. In contrast, accrediting journalists to a one-off event may take weeks to complete. Inevitably the organizers will face some kind of selection process to keep numbers within reasonable limits (this is in itself often a contentious issue), and a certain amount of vetting may also take place before passes and other documentation are issued.

134

EMBASSY OF THE DEMOCRATIC REPUBLIC OF NEWLAND
ЬIЉЙ ЬЧ ᾱя ᶂ ЙђѠѲйІЯᴐ ᶊή̃ᖵкβᶈ⤢ Ю ᴲ ⴲЁ**Ŧ**A⅄Ю

Mr/Mrs/Ms . . . .

Place of Birth . . . .

Date of Birth . . . . Nationality . . . .

Permanent Address . . . .

Occupation . . . .

Business Address . . . .

	Regular		
Passport	Official	No: . . . . Issued at: . . . .
	Diplomatic	

On . . . . Purpose of Journey . . . .

Border of Entry . . . . Means of Transport . . . .

Approx Date of   Duration   If previous visit made
Arrival in Newland: . . . .   of Stay . . . .   to Newland give date . . . .

Places you intend to visit in Newland: . . . .

Accompanied by: . . . .

I undertake not to take into or out of Newland more than Newlandies 500. (Minimum of £100 capital or its equivalent required for entry.)

Date . . . . Signature . . . .

ACCREDITATION AND DOCUMENTATION

Thousands of camera crews and journalists representing news organizations from all over the world now flock to important international events. As a matter of routine many countries demand full personal details of those seeking to enter to undertake assignments, and official accreditation is often required as part of a visa application process. Admission is not guaranteed.

Getting the Story is Often Simpler than Getting into Position

News conferences
One of the most popular modern means of passing newsworthy information to a wide range of media outlets at the same time is to call a news conference. This is a useful short cut for those who wish to avoid the tedium of repeating exactly the same thing to a succession of different people, and while journalists always prefer to deal with stories on an individual basis, news conferences of both the regular and ad hoc variety have come to be accepted as just another source of material. They have also become weapons in the armoury of the news manipulators, who can control the invitations, choose time and place to suit the most accommodating and, if they are so minded, manage the content. In the end the media must make their own decisions about what is newsworthy, but politicians – or more likely the 'spin-doctors' behind them – shrewdly offer a news conference or nothing, and take the opportunity (often during election campaigns) to set the agenda, choosing the subject matter, providing the main speakers, selecting only sympathetic journalists to ask questions from the audience, and restricting the time available for questions.

News conference procedures
A news conference typically follows a set pattern. The 'information-givers' sit on a platform at the front of a large room or hall, and the 'information-receivers' make up an audience facing them. Camera crews are probably banished to the back. The lighting is often inadequate and the acoustics poor. Do not leave anything to chance: arrive early to ensure the best camera position and sound facilities. Most news conferences begin with a speech from the chair, but you probably will not want to shoot it all, as it is unlikely you will know which passages are worth recording. The text is sometimes made available in advance as 'hand-outs': if so, either make your own decision or take the advice of an editorial colleague. But remember that is no guarantee of success, as politicians in particular tend to depart from set texts.

Questions and answers
The second stage in the news conference is usually the free-for-all question and answer session, controlled from the chair. If you are with a journalist from your own organization it is essential to record his or her question and the following answer. Try to get near enough to ensure you have a warning when the question is about to be asked, and it is always worth getting wide shots of the platform and audience to use as cutaways and voice-over material.

Finally, if your reporter is having difficulty getting a question answered, it may well be that he or she is being subjected to one of a number of well-known shut-out ploys, whereby speakers ignore those likely to ask something awkward, use the hubbub as an excuse for not hearing and call 'plants' in the audience to ask soft questions.

136

NEWS CONFERENCES

A way for organizations and individuals to answer questions from or provide
information to a wide range of media outlets at the same time. The intention is
often to avoid the need for a series of repetitive interviews. Try to arrive early for a
good camera position. (Courtesy of the United States Department of Defense.)

Don't Let Others Take Advantage of Who or What you Know

Matters of security

Among the inescapable facts of life over the past 20 years has been that in almost every corner of the world the personal safety of public figures has become a matter of concern. Democratic societies are torn between the need to protect these people while allowing normality to be maintained, but for those involved in attempting to cover their activities, one inevitable consequence has been the steady erosion of freedom of movement. Most journalists reluctantly recognize the need for security arrangements, but you will often find them frustratingly bureaucratic.

Sensible precautions

Alongside your professional duties goes your responsibility as a citizen; therefore it is reasonable to expect you not to do anything which, even unwittingly, would allow others to take advantage of who and what you know. Those determined on mischief or worse have their own means of finding information which will help them carry out their activities: your duty, whatever your personal views, is to avoid making it easier for them. So, where prominent politicians, business people and other VIPs or their families are concerned:

- try not to film car registration numbers
- don't provide obvious clues to where they live
- don't go out of your way to identify security people

Delays and passes

Formal identification documents, obtained in advance, have become requirements for even the most routine events. Issued passes sometimes restrict media access to specific times or areas (the motive is not always directly connected with security) and even then there are inevitable delays when going into meetings or boarding aircraft, for example, so always make a point of arriving with plenty of time to spare. Expect you and your equipment to be searched thoroughly. Sensitive X-ray machines will scan your precious cassettes, but the modern ones will not affect the electronic image. Develop a patient attitude with officials who seem bent on making life difficult for you: however irritating they may be, remember that among the lives they are being paid to protect is yours.

Protecting your sources

Equally, the pressure has never been greater on journalists to soft-pedal on controversial issues or to reveal their sources of information. Journalists have been heavily fined or sent to prison for contempt of court for refusing to reveal the source of information they have published. As a camera-operator you will inevitably be drawn into circumstances in which your contributor will refuse to appear unless guaranteed anonymity (perhaps by some electronic means), and the difficulty here may be in justifying your agreement to other people (see page 170).

OBSTACLES TO NEWS-GATHERING

The reality of modern political life. The need to protect politicians and other public figures from physical harm inevitably has an effect on camera crews going about their normal, everyday news-gathering activities. Downing Street, the home of the British Prime Minister, once freely accessible to all, now has police on guard at the entrance, security gates and ramps.

Guessing Wrongly which Street is 'Safe' Could Prove Fatal

Awkward places
Such is the nature of news, anyone involved in the business of gathering material for TV is inevitably going to get shot at – metaphorically and literally. The reason is obvious, if regrettable: if they are to inform the viewing audience accurately, journalists and camera crews have to be in the front line, witnessing at first hand what is happening. For that reason, repressive regimes intent on keeping their own people in ignorance find ways of ensuring the opportunity to report freely is denied or restricted (see page 142), and this is why camera crews are sometimes singled out for harsh treatment by wrongdoers determined not to let their misdeeds be recorded on video.

War zones
Until you have considerable experience, you will almost certainly find it easier to undertake 'war' coverage from the 'official' side, who are likely to provide accreditation (see page 134), a means of getting to the action, and suitably credible escorts. There are two main drawbacks. First, you will have to agree to their terms, probably including submission to some form of censorship. Secondly, the subtleties of editorial freedom and news-gathering logistics are inclined to be lost on 'the opposition', to whom from then on you may become *persona non grata*. This is because they will not recognize the argument that it is entirely possible to cover an event from one side without actually supporting it. (The same is true, of course, when the situations are reversed, and you find yourself in the company of the 'rebels'.)

Riots and civil disobedience
It is not unusual for camera people to say the 'old-fashioned wars' were easier to cover. At least, they'd say, you knew whose army was whose. The difficulty with the modern manifestation of armed struggle is that it is more likely to be between irregulars rather than military machines, factions rather than countries, so identifying which side is which, and which streets are safe in Belfast or Beirut, is or was sometimes impossible. And guessing wrong can prove fatal.

It is essential not to go rushing into situations without sensible planning. Take your time to build up contacts whom you feel able to trust and are sure you are trustworthy. If you do go out on a dangerous assignment, take precautions (see opposite).

Never allow your presence with a camera to precipitate trouble which otherwise would not occur. Stone-throwing mobs can delight in their activities being shown on television. You do not want to have it on your conscience that you have contributed to death or injury. Try to look down on the action from a vantage point from which you won't attract attention.

CAMERAWORK AS A DANGEROUS PROFESSION

Mohammed Amin, one of the world's outstanding ENG cameramen, with his false lower arm fitted after injury in Addis Ababa, Ethiopia. He was covering an explosion and fire at an ammunition dump. A sound recordist was killed in the same incident. At least 60 journalists died violently in 1992. (Courtesy of Debbie Gaiger, Camerapix.)

Don't Risk Prison or Deportation

Unwelcoming countries
At the last count (1991) the magazine *Index on Censorship* calculated that no more than about a third of the world's countries exercised what could be called 'press freedom'. Part of the outcome is that a depressingly wide range of important countries and events within them are inadequately reported.

Going as a 'tourist'
The description 'journalist' in any passport which still requires identification by occupation is often by itself enough to provoke, at best, lack of co-operation by sensitive immigration officials at the point of entry, and as a result world TV organizations have been known to resort to the subterfuge of equipping staff with second passports and miniature cameras before sending them on assignment as tourists. The introduction of the 'Hi8' video system has made it easier technically to achieve success, but enough 'tourists' have been deported or arrested on suspicion of spying to suggest this clandestine approach should be reserved for very special occasions only.

Preparations
Most preparations for working in other countries are straightforward and obvious, but it is surprising how often they may be overlooked, especially by inexperienced travellers:

- find out in advance whether you need a visa for the country you intend to visit
- make sure your passport is valid long enough for you to complete the assignment and return home
- check whether your arrival bearing a passport with immigration/ emigration stamps from other countries will cause you to be delayed or barred from entry
- be alive to local medical requirements
- be careful not to infringe local currency regulations, especially on departure

Working with 'minders'
You may sometimes be allowed to operate in a foreign country as long as you follow strict rules. These are likely to include maintaining contact with officials at a government department who will in turn provide 'minders', whose main responsibility is to accompany you to ensure that coverage of places and people reflect only the positive aspects of the regime for which they work. The minders may also vet the material you shoot or submit it to a separate censor. Although this can be an extremely annoying and frustrating, experienced crews know the best way of achieving success is by adopting a consistently conciliatory and friendly approach, especially to regular minders, who may become bored with their duties and more likely to let contentious material pass.

SENSIBLE PRECAUTIONS FOR AWKWARD PLACES

- Keep your inoculations and vaccinations up to date
- Have suitable clothing: be prepared for marked changes in temperature and weather
- Always have comfortable footwear. You may have to walk or march long distances
- If in doubt take 24 hours' supply of emergency rations
- Carry a small first-aid kit: bandages, sticky plasters, antiseptic lotion, scissors
- Carry tablets for water purification, anti-malaria and anti-diarrhoea
- If possible, carry fresh water, especially in the tropics. Don't forget toilet rolls
- Where you have no transport, carry all the above in a sturdy back-pack, along with spare tapes, batteries and equipment
- In war: don't wander off alone and become isolated. You could become a prisoner
- In inter-communal unrest: get to know the various factions and their territory: if they want coverage they will look after you

The Difference between the 'Front' and 'Feature' Pages

Current affairs
The historical distinction between 'news' and 'current affairs' which is still recognized in some broadcasting organizations is a peculiar one. To the outsiders and other professional journalists who accept no such demarcation the concept is outmoded: all 'news' is simply 'news', and they are unable to see any difference.

The definition of current affairs
To those who continue to cling to it, the distinction can be defined as a matter of editorial philosophy, and they use as an analogy the difference between a newspaper's front page and its feature articles inside. There is a clear difference, they maintain, between the straightforward gathering and transmission of facts and the more discursive examination and interpretation of them. It is a compelling argument at a time when it is more difficult than ever for newspaper readers to distinguish facts from opinion.

But nothing is set in concrete and the lines are frequently blurred, with each side liable to stray – knowingly or unknowingly – into the others' territory. Even current affairs and hard news practitioners from the same stable are therefore not immune to what is known as 'creative tension'.

Camera crews are likely to fall into the same broad categories: there are those whose preference for the quick, direct approach lends itself to hard news, and those who are better qualified for the slightly slower pace of current affairs. The more deeply a subject is examined, the greater the likelihood it will take up more air time, but 'current affairs' is less to do with duration than approach. Current affairs items tend to be issue led, to add gloss or provide a deeper understanding of events behind the headlines.

Some crews will of course find themselves caught in the middle of the argument, for although there is usually an intention to match like with like, there are inevitably occasions when 'news' teams find themselves on 'current affairs' stories, and vice versa.

Backgrounders
A backgrounder is often an amalgam of archive and new footage. Typically they are interpretive or explanatory items which set out to put news items into context: film profiles of public figures; prepared obituaries made up of historical material and specially filmed 'tributes'; reports made in anticipation of events held for broadcast until they occur – the conclusion of a trial, for example. ENG camera crews are very likely to be involved, not necessarily in the whole item, but as contributors of small pieces to a jigsaw puzzle.

NEWS OR CURRENT AFFAIRS: HOW COVERAGE DIFFERS

'Village bypass' story: The official opening by a Government minister of a new section of trunk road. It bypasses a village containing several buildings of national historical interest which have been undermined by years of heavy through traffic towards a port 15 miles away. Accidents and other hold-ups have also recently increased, leading to a decision by one of the main shipping companies to threaten to switch their business elsewhere. The road cuts through a nearby beauty spot and conservation area. Protests are expected from environmentalists who lost a lengthy legal battle to have the road diverted at greater cost, but supporters from the village lobbied successfully for the bypass to be built and are also expected to be out in numbers to celebrate.

This is how each area might tackle the subject:

EARLY-EVENING NEWS

Editorial value: conflict of interests between two groups of people, both of which have a strong case. Coverage to illustrate what the problem is and the strength of feeling which exists. Edited duration: 2 minutes 15 seconds

Content:
Scenes of police keeping apart vociferous opposing factions as the minister arrives to conduct the official opening (20 seconds)

Ministerial speech and tape-cutting: first convoy drives through (followed by camera car) (30 seconds)

Interview with leader of protest movement (20 seconds)

Exteriors of now-tranquil village high street including shots of affected buildings (20 seconds)

Interview with leader of village support movement (20 seconds)

Reporter piece to camera on bridge overlooking fast-flowing traffic on bypass (25 seconds), summing up the problem, including the potential economic effect on the port. Total edited duration: 2 minutes 15 seconds

LATE-EVENING CURRENT AFFAIRS

Editorial value: conflict of interest between two groups, one of which has been seeking to improve the quality of life of the local population, the other to retain unscarred an area of natural beauty, and the side issue of the effect on the local port. Duration: 10 minutes

Content:
Pre-shot pictures of countryside, emphasizing its beauty (30 seconds)

Pre-shot pictures of port activity (45 seconds)

Pre-shot pictures of ancient village buildings with articulated lorries driving through; close-ups of damage to brickwork and foundations (45 seconds)

Pre-shot piece to camera by reporter at scene of bypass workings (1 minute)

Scenes at opening ceremony (15 seconds)

Studio interview with leaders of the two factions (6 minutes 45 seconds)

145

Documentaries are Not Necessarily Very Lengthy

Beyond hard news

If every comedian wants to play Hamlet, then it is fair to assume that (nearly) every ENG cameraman wants to try his/her hand at something more substantial than hard news. Not everyone can do it successfully: years of paring coverage to the bone to meet the exacting requirements of daily deadlines take their mental and physical toll, and some find – much to their surprise and disappointment – that much as they like the idea of variety, they lack the patience or range of technique needed for different format assignments.

Documentaries

Documentaries usually cover single subjects, either as programmes in their own right or as elements of others. There is no rule covering how long a documentary must be to be classed as such: some of the most effective run no more than four or five minutes. What we are considering here, though, is a structure more likely to lend itself to a minimum of a quarter of an hour if it is going to make any real impact on the viewing audience.

The team

Documentary projects are usually led by directors or producers who exercise complete control over the artistic, editorial, financial and logistical details. The rest of the team may consist of an assistant director, production manager, production assistant and reporter/presenter. A single camera crew is the norm, though the basic camera-operator/recordist/lighting assistant will sometimes be supported by a camera assistant and second sound recordist or electrician.

Documentary director-cameramen are by no means unheard of, and the aim of being in sole charge of a prestige production is a most attractive one, but newcomers will learn considerably more at this stage from being part of a team under a competent and experienced director.

Preparation: 'the recce'

Good documentaries are constructed to follow a narrative which makes the best use of story-line, location, commentary and camerawork. Thorough preparation and research of the subject and participants are essential ingredients. From the camera team's point of view, the most important element is 'the recce' (reconaissance) – one or several preparatory visits made by the director to the location of the shoot. A recce may take weeks, days or just a few hours according to the nature of the subject. But the purpose remains the same – to establish at first hand the most suitable sites and angles for shots and to try to anticipate any practical problems which might arise when work starts. On some rare occasions the cameraman may be allowed the luxury of joining a recce. If asked and available – go.

146

① GV of stately home

② Zoom in to doorway

③ Continue zoom as open doors reveal reporter

④ End zoom as reporter starts piece to camera

STORY-BOARDS

. . . are sketches prepared by directors when planning how shots will link on screen. A very useful device in the preparatory stage of documentary-making, especially if the camera team is able to see them before shooting. Story-boards may cover whole assignments or only the more difficult scenes.

Preparation is the Key to Success in Documentary-making

Documentary preparation

Although the recce may well be considered to be the most crucial pre-production stage in documentary-making, the first step is actually the treatment. This is a fuller and more comprehensive version of the often-sketchy news Assignment Sheet (see page 167) and sets out in written form details of the director's purpose, proposed content, how it is to be achieved and how long it will take to make.

Shooting scripts

As a result of the recce and before the shoot takes place the director prepares a written shooting script, listing in chronological order which scenes are to be shot. This is very rarely the order in which they will be edited together. The aim is to ensure economy of time and effort for everyone involved. Imagine, for example, the final version of the documentary is to include two separate interviews shown several minutes apart but shot using similar backgrounds on the same location. The purpose of the shooting script is to ensure that the two interviews are arranged to be recorded consecutively: this saves the entire team an unnecessary and time-consuming return to the same spot.

Schedules and story-boards

An adjunct to the shooting script is the shooting schedule, which provides details of the time and places where shooting is to take place. The schedule is likely to include notice of travel arrangements, rendezvous details, contact names and addresses, an indication of working hours, meal-break plans and so on.

As an aid to planning, the director may also use a story-board, a series of sketches showing how each shot is intended to look and how it links with the next.

Docu-dramas

Not to be confused with the commonly accepted definition of 'documentary' is the recent phenomenon known as 'docu-drama', which uses known facts as the basis for film/studio reconstructions of important or controversial historical and political events. Actors are employed to play the parts of the real-life personalities involved, using court transcripts, official records, published or unpublished memoirs, etc., as the sources for their lines. It is the interpretation of these facts, and the assumptions made about the inevitable gaps between what is known and what is not, which often leads to controversy, and the use of genuine archive footage sometimes mixed with specially shot, simulated archive footage at times adds to the confusion in viewers' minds.

```
THE ROAD TO RUIN: VILLAGE BY-PASS SEQUENCE: SHOOTING SCHEDULE

Crewing:                Director: Jack Leon
                        Reporter: Cynthia Goodwin
                        PA: Carol Winston
                        Assistant: Pat Landau
                        Sound: Alan Solomon
                        Lights: Peter Mann

Wednesday, September 15:
RV 1130:                Horse & Jockey,
                        47 High Street
                        Little Elmfield
                        Suffolk.

Directions:
M11 to Junction 10, then A11/A45 towards Stowmarket. A1120/B1079
to Great/Little Elmfield. Distance from London approx 75 miles.

Schedule:
1200:  set & light for interview with District Councillor Paul
Zatz, landlord of the Horse & Jockey, who has led the successful
campaign for the by-pass.  Location: Village (main) Bar

1330:  Lunch at Horse & Jockey (Writing Room)

1445: exterior interview with the Rev. William Baynes, Vicar of
St.Agnes, the 14th century church damaged by heavy lorries.
Location: Lych Gate (s.e. corner)

1615: Tea break (details to be arranged)

1645:  exteriors church, High Street, other historic buildings.

1830: wrap

Accommodation: Horse & Jockey (details with Carol)

Script conference: (Room 4) 2130 (to be confirmed)
```

```
THE ROAD TO RUIN: VILLAGE BY-PASS SEQUENCE: SHOOTING SCRIPT

DATE        SHOT NO.            DESCRIPTION

15/9        1.          BCU articulated lorry (from St.Agnes
                        Church tower), zooming out to GV High
                        Street,
                        Little Elmfield

            2.          MS on-coming traffic through street

            3.          LS Cynthia on traffic island

            4.          MCU Cynthia piece to camera (approx 45
                        sec.) (To be scripted)
                        ending with voice-over

            5.          LS pan down exterior St.Agnes church,
                        voice-over

            6.          MS walking shot of Rev. William Baynes into

            7.          MCU interview
```

BEYOND HARD NEWS

Documentaries may include coverage of current events as part of an examination
of wider issues. A history of decline of the railways, entitled 'The Road to Ruin',
might use the Village Bypass Row to help illustrate the subject. Custom and
practice calls for a bigger crew and more formal, detailed planning for a project
which could take several weeks to shoot.

The More you Like the Game, the Better your Coverage

Covering sport
Watching sport has become one of the most popular leisure activities in every part of the world reached by TV. The football World Cup, the Olympic Games and the other outstanding international events draw audiences which can be counted in hundreds of millions. Television organizations spend vast sums on securing the rights which will allow them to spend more money committing specialist staff and equipment on covering every possible angle for hour after hour of prime-time transmission.

Sport as news
Sport is also news. Not just because of Heysal or Hillsborough, but because editors have come to recognize that sporting action sometimes fights its way into a bulletin on its own editorial merits. Many news programmes also reserve regular slots to report sports news and events. In either case, any ENG crew may expect to be rostered to cover a sporting item just as they are assigned to a protest march or political news conference. That means no multi-camera units, no specially erected podiums: only a single camera operated by a minimum crew.

Getting to know the rules
The best commentators are those who have a deep understanding and affection for their chosen sport. The very unpredictable nature of news means this cannot always be so for the camera crew, but at least a working knowledge of and liking for this kind of work will ease the task.

When assigned to a sport alien to you, try to enlist the help of an expert to identify the personalities involved and advise you on some of the basic rules likely to influence the flow of the action.

Before the game
Try to reconnoitre the venue to locate the best camera position or positions. It will pay off. For example, when covering a football or rugby match in western Europe in the winter you will find the sun low in the sky, and the camera lens will possibly be subjected to rain sweeping in on the prevailing wind. Aim for a position under cover on the western side of the ground, so the setting sun and winds are behind the camera. Planning will also enable you to investigate the availability of a mains power supply if coverage is likely to be extended.

Think also about your ability to get your material back to base. If you do not have the luxury of a microwave or satellite link to transmit your signals and have to rely on old-fashioned methods, remember that the deserted stadium in which you set up your camera will probably become a huge excited throng, choking the streets with their cars – and blocking the vehicle you had parked two hours earlier. If necessary, arrange for a messenger to ferry the tape, making sure in advance he knows exactly where to meet you.

150

The right way:
camera mounted
on a gantry high in
the grandstand

The wrong way:
camera looking west into the setting sun
and open to the elements

SOCCER AND RUGBY COVERAGE

The right and wrong positions from which to cover winter-time soccer and rugby
matches.

Number One Rule: Keep your Eye on the Ball!

Following the action
Some sports consist of intermittent explosions of violent action: others are conducted at a leisurely and measured pace. Sometimes the ball, puck or shuttlecock is continually in motion, up and down, end to end, side to side. Sometimes only the competitors move. Such is the variety it is difficult to give clear-cut advice, so the few guidelines which follow are intended to apply only to the most popular sports.

And here the Number One rule is

- Keep your eye on the ball: in other words, keep the ball in frame.
- Be aware what is happening outside the frame. Draft your recordist or reporter as a second pair of eyes.
- Sustained coverage of sports events using the standard ENG side viewfinder inhibits panning movements and is very tiring on the eyes. Use a 5-inch (127mm) or similar size monitor, mounted on a camera, to eliminate these problems. It will also give you the freedom to look briefly beyond the viewfinder without upsetting the continuity of coverage.

Wide angles and close-ups
- Limit your use of the wide-angle shot. It will leave the audience wondering what is happening. Your aim should be to allow the viewer to follow the action, see the ball clearly and identify the players.
- Close-ups, so effective in multi-camera sports coverage, present difficulties for the single camera covering the action, as the ball suddenly disappears out of frame and it may take a critical second or two to relocate it. Conversely, a continuous general view can quickly become boring, so do find time to shoot close-ups of participants.

Cutaways
Cutaways, usually shot during breaks in play, are an essential ingredient for the picture editor, as they act as useful bridges with which to telescope time or action. Do not ignore spectators or coaches sitting on the sidelines, remembering that the shots have to be consistent with what is taking place. A cutaway of a crowd waiting quietly for the end of an interval between sets of tennis is not going to help a picture editor trying to telescope a display of tantrums at the umpire's chair.

Make sure what you offer is a variety.

Soccer and rugby
In soccer or rugby, where play is moving from left to right, aim to keep the ball on a line about one-third in from the left of frame. This leaves you the rest of the frame in which to anticipate the long pass forward or the 'up and under'. If the play is moving in the opposite direction, keep the ball on a line about one-third in from the right.

152

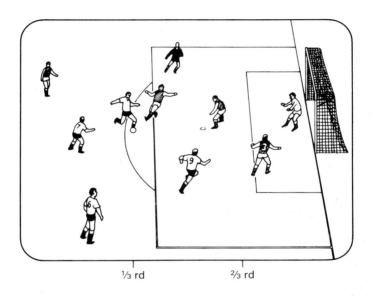

⅓ rd   ⅔ rd

COVERING A MOVING BALL GAME

Where play is moving from left to right, aim to keep the ball on a line about one-third in from the left of frame. This will also allow you to anticipate a sudden change of direction.

Don't Let your Quest for Shots Upset the Competitors

Cricket and other sports
Cricket is an especially difficult sport to cover and a 5-inch (127mm) viewfinder is essential. The best camera position is above the action and about in line with the wickets. To move more than 45 degrees (roughly the equivalent of the 'first slip' position – see diagram opposite) outside it will be unsatisfactory, and with the camera 90 degrees to the wicket it would be impossible to see the 'fast ball'. Similarly, the speed at which the ball leaves the bat is often too quick to follow. A brief look outside the viewfinder can help locate the ball and redeem the coverage, at least in part.

Lawn tennis
This presents fewer problems, as all the action is confined within a limited space. The best position is an elevated one in the middle of one end of the court. Your biggest mistake would be to set up centrally, opposite the net, which would mean swinging the camera from side to side to follow the ball.

Golf
Unlike most other sports, golf has a moving 'gallery', and during big tournaments it is all too easy to be caught up with or mistaken for spectators. So make sure you and your recordist have all the right accreditation and identification to facilitate your coverage. Most tournament courses offer motorized buggies for hire. These vehicles are ideal for carrying your equipment over miles of fairway, although there are bound to be some areas where they are not allowed. The recordist should drive, allowing the camera operator to follow the action on foot.

In general, keep a careful record of your coverage: in the editing suite it can be difficult to distinguish one patch of rough from another.

The best shots from the tee or fairway are from behind the player, allowing the camera to follow the ball in flight. The exceptions are the short holes. International-class players will reach the green in one, so from a position near the hole you should be able to follow play from the tee-shot to the moment the ball lands on line with the pin.

Sprints – humans and horses
The best you can hope for is probably an elevated position, a steady tripod and a slow pan following the runners towards the winning post. Head-on shots looking back along the track, although sometimes dramatic, give no sense of the distance between competitors, but the opportunity of shooting through the sun-roof of a car driving parallel to the runners should not be missed.

Keeping out of the way
Finally, be alive to the needs of those taking part in competitive sport – for most it's their profession:

- don't encroach on playing areas
- don't cause distractions by careless movement, equipment noise or your shadow

154

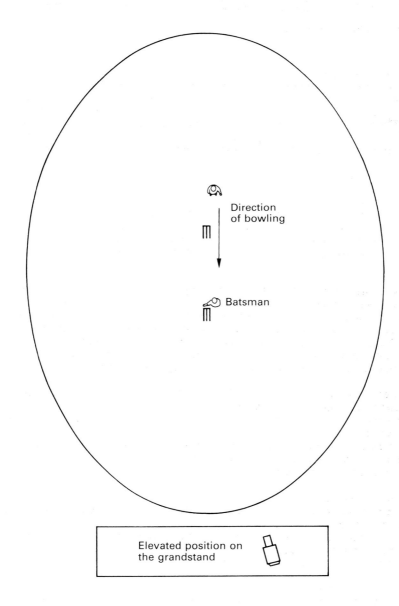

Direction
of bowling

Batsman

Elevated position on
the grandstand

CRICKET

The best camera position is elevated at an angle of about 5 degrees and no more than 15 degrees to the line of the wickets. A wider or narrow angle view will be unsuitable.

155

Other People, Other Jobs – 1

Get to know what your colleagues do
For many a young aspirant concentrating on taking the first hesitant steps towards the chosen career as a fully-fledged ENG camera-operator, how colleagues go about their own professional business is of fleeting if any interest. But even in the days of improved technology and scaled-down staffs, TV still leans heavily on teamwork. The more you learn about the role of others in the team, the more you will come to understand the importance of your own part in it. And as the concept of multi-skilling takes hold, the ability to assimilate complementary skills should not be minimized. It does not mean trying to take someone else's job from them.

Directing
Directors on location are the creative leaders of film projects, so they need sound managerial and organizational skills, as well as 'artistic' ability. Some directors combine the role of cameraman; others have *been* cameramen or picture editors, and any experience they have previously gained in some other capacity is clearly advantageous, but it is not always an easy move. Some directors get by despite their shortcomings as managers of people, but the best achieve what they want by strength of personality as much as by their creative instincts, fostering a team spirit which brings the best out of the people around them.

Studio work is altogether more technical, and in many ways more taxing, despite the controlled environment in which the directors work. News programmes remain among the few which are still broadcast live, adding to the pressure on the director. Although automated systems may have begun to relieve the burden, for the most part directors can expect to be captain of a production team and in control of technical facilities which are likely to include three or four cameras, pre-recorded videotape on separate machines, electronic graphics and stills stores, and remote studios.

It ought to be that all directors are capable of working effectively both on location and in the studio, but this is not always the case.

Producing
Producing and directing roles are sometimes combined, sometimes not, so it is not surprising to find confusion over the distinction, where it exists. In simple terms, the *producer* is likely to have editorial and financial responsibility for one or a number of programmes, including the choice of production team and director, who is charged with the artistic interpretation of the content.

Much depends on the size and structure of the organization concerned, which may be complex enough to have the producer reporting to an *executive producer* or *series editor* with overall control.

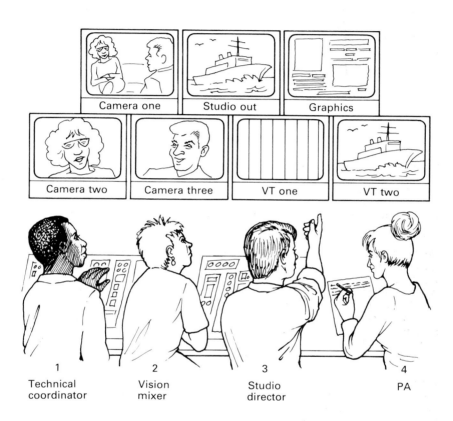

Camera one · Studio out · Graphics

Camera two · Camera three · VT one · VT two

1
Technical
coordinator

2
Vision
mixer

3
Studio
director

4
PA

STUDIO DIRECTION

News-related programmes are among the few still transmitted live. Studio control rooms (sometimes known as 'Galleries') are usually staffed by a technical co-ordinator/engineer (1) who is responsible for technical facilities and quality; a vision mixer (2) who selects from the picture sources available to the programme; a studio director (3) who leads the production team and is the artistic interpreter of editorial wishes; and a production assistant (4) who generally supports the director with timing of scripts and sequences. A sound supervisor, responsible for mixing and monitoring the sound from the studio, may be separately sited.

157

Other People, Other Jobs – 2

Writers and writing
The combination of camera and writing skills is not unknown in small-station TV, where quality has to come second to the necessity of economic survival, and staff simply have to turn their hand to anything. Even under less pressing circumstances, an understanding of basic writing techniques is invaluable for anyone involved in the gathering of news, and those whose first task is to operate the camera should see how others do it and then try it for themselves.

Matching words to pictures
The mechanics of writing material for TV are few and very straightforward, and anyone with a moderate grasp of language should be able to turn out passable scripts within a few hours. The accepted formula of three (English) words of commentary to every second of pictures has been tested and proved accurate by generations of initially sceptical news-writers. What distinguishes the *good* writer from the merely adequate is the use she or he makes of the accompanying illustration.

The Number One rule is that words and pictures must be made to complement each other: if they do not, there is only one winner – the viewer is easily distracted by the power of the picture, and the commentary, however important, will be lost. But neither must the two be tied so closely together that the words only repeat what the viewer sees. The script should be used to convey information which adds to understanding, and this applies as much to the news item lasting 30 seconds as to the hour-long documentary.

Keeping it simple
The other main message is that sentences should be kept short and the language simple, direct and conversational. If scripts read aloud sound stilted or over-complicated they should be changed.

Language use
If news programmes are to be bias-free, the words used should be neutral, not value-laden. Traps for the novice writer include casually accepted sexist and other language which listeners may find offensive, and extra care is necessary to avoid the legal minefields through which experienced journalists tread with delicacy. Among the most important laws affecting writers are Libel, the purpose of which is to protect reputations from unfair attack; Copyright, laying down rules for the use of material owned by other authors; and Contempt, which covers the reporting of crime to ensure that anyone accused is able to receive a fair trial (see page 168).

Natural sound
Finally, the best writers remember that TV is two-dimensional: it is about sound as well as pictures. Especially with short items, the temptation is to cover every frame with commentary. If good natural sound is available, pauses should be built in to allow scripts to 'breathe'.

page	title	Tue May 7 13:11 content	writer	dur
015	BYPASS	JANE + CAM 1 + MAP	BH	0:23

JANE I/V_____/Residents of a 14th century village in Suffolk
have been celebrating the opening of a new
bypass for which they've been campaigning for
more than ten years. But today's ceremony
just outside
MAP (SUFFOLK, ELMFIELD)__/Little Elmfield was marred by protests.
Environmentalists who say the
ANIMATE BYPASS ROUTE____/new road cuts through an area of outstanding
natural beauty, blocked the way as the
minister for transport arrived. Our reporter
Tim Smith was there.
VT (BYPASS) FOLLOWS   VT
[DUR: 0:23"]

WRITING FOR TELEVISION

Scripts for news programmes tend to be written on word-processors as
newsroom computer systems supersede typewriters. Page identification includes
story title and writer. Scripts must follow the convention that technical
instructions appear on the left-hand side of the page, text on the right.

Other People, Other Jobs – 3

Producers and performers
As the complexity of broadcasting has grown, so has the responsibility of those working in it, and the majority of journalists in TV newsrooms who were previously classed as sub-editors or writers now find themselves called *assistant producers* or *producers* according to seniority.

The change in title reflects both the break with newspaper technology and the broader range of duties they are expected to undertake. Writing has come to represent a very small part of a producer's work, the bulk of it being made up of organizing human and technical resources for one or more items within a news programme. Producers may be generalists or concentrate on specialist subjects. Field producers ply a similar trade, but out on assignment away from the newsroom. In some organizations, producers may also be responsible for entire programmes: in others, they are likely to be known as editors.

Researchers
Researchers tend to be graded lower than producers, although the job is similar in many ways. Even though researchers may write and direct – either on location or in the studio – their main task is usually to amass the raw material from which programmes or programme elements can be made.

Researchers gather facts, collect archive material, find the right people to interview, suggest lines of questioning or perhaps conduct the interviews themselves – in short, they mastermind all the preparation needed for others to use.

Anchors
Of all the jobs in TV journalism, the most glamorous are those of reporter or *presenter (anchor)*. The best-known names and faces are those who appear regularly on screen. The leading anchors of daily live news programmes are regarded as the super-stars, and the enormous and continuing public interest that their on- and off-screen lives generate reaches near soccer transfer-style hysteria when they change employers.

The term 'anchor' accurately reflects the responsibility their pivotal role demands of them, and whatever effort goes on behind the scenes, the fickle viewing public inevitably equates a programme's success or failure with their highly subjective opinion of the person fronting it. It was not many years ago that anchors were known as newsreaders, and were chosen primarily for the way they looked and spoke rather than for any journalistic ability. Today it is rare to find an anchorman or woman who does not have a solid background as a reporter or correspondent. The modern communications technology which is capable of bringing raw events straight on to the screen requires the high levels of instinctive judgement which only journalistic experience can supply.

Attends programme meetings

Selects archive material

Researches given item

Commissions graphics

Briefs reporter

Supervises picture-editing

Writes link for presenter/reporter

WHAT A PRODUCER DOES

Producers (or their junior counterparts) are usually responsible for segments of news-related programmes. Their role once reflected that of the print sub-editor, whose work was very similar. The change in title has taken place simultaneously with the development of their duties to embrace editorial production as well as writing. They are also increasingly responsible for the financial control of their activities.

Other People, Other Jobs – 4

Reporters and reporting
Anchors/presenters apart, the most glamorous editorial job in TV is that of *reporter*. This is the basic level of location news-gatherer for those organizations which make the distinction between desk- based and field-based operations staff.

The reporter's role
Crew levels generally have not yet reached the stage at which the camera-operator's role is integrated into the reporters', or vice versa, so for the moment at least the reporter has managerial and editorial responsibility for the team in the field. (Leadership of an assignment may also be assumed by a producer if one is involved.) Correspondents – more senior reporters (see page 164) – tend to be 'self-starters' on specialist subjects, whereas general reporters are assigned to stories as they arise, rather like taxis picking up fare-paying passengers. Preparation is often cursory and done on the hoof. Some reporters are paired with camera crews on a semi-permanent basis, but others simply join crews on location and go their separate ways after each assignment.

What a reporter does
Reporting calls for the ability to work fast, and have sound editorial judgement, good writing skills, all-round understanding of television, an acceptable screen presence, a suitable microphone voice and plenty of self-confidence. Reporters' duties fall into three main technical categories:

- interviewing
- pieces to camera ('stand-uppers')
- voice-over (commentary) writing

These can be undertaken separately or constructed into 'packages' in any combination, live or recorded, on location or in the studio. Good technique is best achieved with specialized training, especially in interviewing technique, which is often regarded as the most difficult and potentially controversial area of a reporter's work. Interviews come in all shapes and sizes, ranging from door-steppers with newsworthy people, through single-question 'spot news' (eyewitness) interviews, to formal set-pieces lasting whole programmes. Stand-uppers in the field demand the ability to compose and deliver short passages convincingly to camera. This is usually done from memory, although electronic and mechanical prompting aids of various sorts are increasingly being employed (see page 94).

Along with camera crews, reporters are in the front line as far as ethical matters are concerned. Viewers and broadcasting watchdog organizations are more sensitive than ever to any activities they regard as intrusive or unfair on the part of TV journalists, and awareness of the problem adds to the pressure on reporters as they go about their business.

Gathers information on the spot

Decides content and shape

Supervises camera crew

Carries out interviews

Records piece to camera

Writes and records voice-over

Maintains base links

WHAT A REPORTER DOES

Reporters in the field are traditionally in charge of camera crews. With single-camera operation the reporter may also be expected to carry out some of the recordist's duties.

Other People, Other Jobs – 5

Correspondents
As a camera-operator engaged in news or current affairs work you are certain to have to work alongside novice reporters who are unsure of their own abilities and look to you for guidance every step of the way. At the other end of the scale, at the top of the career ladder for reporters, come *correspondents* – commanding figures, vastly experienced and knowledgeable.

The specialist
The term 'correspondent' is usually applied to any senior reporter charged with the responsibility of covering a specialist subject such as politics, economics, social affairs and science. Unlike general reporters, who probably appear on duty rosters to cover 'diary' stories, correspondents are given the latitude to generate their own material from their inside knowledge of the issues and personalities involved in their specialist field. With intelligent use, even a small network of correspondents should be able to provide a news organization with a consistently up-to-date picture of developments in a number of key areas, together with a steady stream of ideas for future coverage.

Foreign correspondents
Another area of specialism is found in the *foreign correspondent*, often regarded as the *crème de la crème* of all reporting jobs. Foreign news-gathering is by far the most expensive operation in TV journalism. While general reporters and correspondents may be sent abroad on short-term 'fire-brigade' assignments, the news organizations which pride themselves on having their own people reporting from the most newsworthy parts of the world invest heavily in basing staff abroad. Only the biggest and most powerful news organizations can afford to commit the funds necessary to have even a handful of staff overseas and these tend to be based in countries with good communications and proven or developing newsworthiness. The rest rely on the international agencies such as Reuters Television (formerly Visnews) and Worldwide Television News (WTN) and the stringers who supply them on a freelance basis.

Foreign bureaux
The cost of running a foreign bureau includes office accommodation, administrative and technical support as well as the necessary domestic arrangements. To help make the operation pay, correspondents are likely to have to cover whole continents from their base, being expected to make forays anywhere on their patch. There is also an increasing tendency for national news organizations who are not strictly in competition to share offices and other facilities in an effort to keep costs down. Bureaux in some of the most important news-gathering centres also have their own resident camera crews, sometimes recruited locally but sometimes also brought in on rotation from base.

Attends specialist group briefings

Reads specialist publications

Makes and maintains specialist contacts

Offers editorial guidance on subject

Undertakes own reports

WHAT A CORRESPONDENT DOES

Correspondents are senior reporters who tend to develop knowledge of specialist subjects. They spend much of their time making use of their contacts to set up their own stories, unlike general reporters who are controlled by assignments editors.

Other People, Other Jobs – 6

Planners and 'The Desk'

If they stopped to think about it, viewers settled down in front of their favourite daily TV news programmes would soon become aware that only a small proportion of the news coverage they were watching was entirely unplanned.

The reason is simple: newsworthy events and the presence of cameras coincide only rarely. For example, the Gulf War of 1991 was covered by camera crews who were already in position before hostilities began, and very little actual fighting was captured by the camera; coverage of natural and man-made disasters and similarly unpredictable happenings tend to show the aftermath rather than the event itself.

The currency of television

Pictures represent the currency of TV, so editors of news programmes have to offer their viewers what amounts to a selection of happenings they are able to predict will take place in front of their camera crews and reporters. It may not always be possible to determine in advance exactly how those pictures will come together and what the editorial value will be, but the result is that the news agenda consists of variations on a fairly limited theme. Among these are the activities of governmental or other leading political and public figures; 'official' reports or statistics; follow-up coverage of recent events; news conferences; court cases; and fixtures in the sporting and social calendar.

Forward planning

In order to meet these commitments, the average TV news organization develops a sophisticated intelligence system designed to ensure that its camera crews and reporters are already in position when the events they wish to cover are about to take place. The result is a remarkable similarity between the products of rival programmes.

The hub of this system is variously known as 'News-gathering', 'Intake', 'Input', 'Assignments', or perhaps just 'The Desk', whose inhabitants run the lives of the teams in the field. In the best-ordered organizations, editorial and technical planning is carried out by a single person or operates side-by-side. Duties may be carried out in either case by a specialist *planner*, or by experienced staff seconded from operational duties. Some cameramen take so naturally to this role they make the transition a permanent one.

The main task of the operational planner is to maintain a roster of sufficient camera crews to cover all eventualities, assign the most appropriate one for each story, ensure all details of an assignment are made available, fix the rendezvous with the reporter and other staff, arrange the collection of security, car parking and other documents which allow coverage to be carried out with a minimum of delay, assess what special equipment might be needed, decide the best way of getting the completed material back to base, and maintain contact with the crew on location to keep abreast of progress.

Assignment no.: 107/93
Story title: Homeless
Camera: David Harris
Reporter: Carole Dobson

Date: June 12
Sound: Mark Hurst

Story details:
Fourteen residents of an old people's home are being made homeless because the terraced council building they moved to a fortnight ago is subsiding. Social service workers are taking them to temporary accommodation.

Coverage:
Exteriors/interiors of building (if possible); interviews with staff; coverage of Social Service workers; interview with Head of Social Services Committee.

Location:
14 Granary Street

RV time:
9 a.m. (staff may not arrive until 10 a.m. approx.)

Contact:
Jackie Gellman (Supervisor). Phone: 1234

Other details:
Parking. Meters only (Wardens very active) or car park in Granary Close (100 yards)

Note: 2-minute item wanted for lunch-time news.

THE DESK

Camera operators and recordists are often given the opportunity to stand in for members of the team who control operation assignments. This may include arranging details for inclusion in camera Assignment Sheets. These may be similar to documentary Shooting Schedules (see page 148), but may also contain less detail.

How Far should you Co-operate with 'Authority'?

The camera and the law

Western society is often said to be all the healthier for the mutual antipathy which exists between 'authority' which seeks to govern (with a big and a small 'g'), often with the maximum of secrecy, and the media, whose purpose is to challenge, to expose. Yet the nature of their separate activities often drives the two sides – however reluctantly – into co-operation, testament to that being the vast information and public relations machinery which exists in most democratic countries to service the demands of broadcasting and the press.

Co-operating with authority

What you may have to decide on occasion is how far that co-operation should go. Journalistic insistence on the public's right to know could in some circumstances lead to the loss of innocent life. What principle is compromised by agreeing to the imposition of a news blackout while a search goes on for the innocent victim of a kidnap plot? Other examples: a camera crew engaged in riot coverage films a rioter attacking a policeman. Should they also film a policeman using excessive force to tackle a rioter? And how far does coverage of terrorist incidents add fuel to the 'oxygen of publicity' argument – a phrase coined by the former British Prime Minister, Margaret Thatcher, in an (unsuccessful) attempt to influence the media to restrain themselves from undertaking any coverage likely to have a positive effect on the morale of terrorists or their supporters.

Legal constraints

There are a number of basic laws affecting anyone involved in news-gathering, and serious study of those outlined below is strongly encouraged:

- Libel, a branch of the law of defamation, exists to protect the reputation of the individual from unjustified attack by anything published (broadcast), though there are a number of defences against any action alleging libel.
- Contempt of Court is aimed at ensuring those accused of criminal offences receive a fair trial. One of the most relevant elements is that photography is not allowed within the court 'precincts', an undefined area which includes the court itself.*
- Trespass straightforwardly seeks to keep camera crews off private property.
- The Official Secrets Act, revised in 1990, makes it an offence to report certain matters connected with security.
- Copyright law, revised in 1988, exists to protect authorship: for example, notice should be taken that anyone interviewed now has the 'moral ownership' of their own words.

---

* Experimental TV coverage of selected court cases has been under active consideration by British legal authorities.

THE CAMERA AND THE LAW

During criminal trials, legal restrictions prevent photography inside a court or anywhere within an ill-defined area known as 'the precincts'. Court backgrounds are favoured settings for reporter pieces-to-camera about important cases, but crews shooting exteriors of any court building, whether the renowned Old Bailey or a suburban magistrates' court are technically breaking the law of contempt. In theory, you cause an obstruction every time you stop to raise your camera in a public place, and the police are within their rights to move you on.

Transmitted Pictures are in the Public Domain

Handing over material
One of the biggest ethical dilemmas regularly confronting TV news organizations arises from the problems which beset modern society. In the course of covering riots, demonstrations and other potentially dangerous situations, camera crews often find themselves witnesses to wrongdoing and with the pictorial evidence to back it up. In some circumstances the possession of such pictures – or only the belief of possession – is sufficient to put their lives or liberty in danger.

The principles
The response to any request concerning the handing over of material for use connected with legal proceedings is based on the fundamental need to protect news-gathering staff and with it the freedom to continue reporting events of public interest. And that would soon cease to exist if people at large believed camera crews were routinely passing to the authorities videotape recordings of their activities. Or as the BBC's guidelines put it: '. . . if those being recorded regard the programme-makers as agents of investigating and prosecuting bodies'.*

The principle is clear enough: what has been edited and transmitted is 'in the public domain', and usually there can be little objection to handing it over. What is much more difficult is when requests are made for the raw, untransmitted material, which may or may not be useful as evidence. In these cases, insistence by the authorities (usually the police and occasionally in the form of highly public 'raids' on broadcasting premises) should be met with an equally firm insistence that the material will be released only as a result of a court order.

Allowing viewings
There are times when a viewing of material will suffice as an alternative to allowing it to be taken away, and in weighing up whether or not to accede to such a request it is important to remember that camera crews and journalists do not stand apart from society. If no principle is breached by collaborating with the authorities, it would be irresponsible not to do so.

Tricky situations
In some circumstances, of course, camera crews find themselves intimidated by people or surroundings in which arguments about the legal niceties of such matters would simply not be appropriate or timely. In these cases, only common sense born of experience will guide your actions. Put simply, no story is worth getting badly injured or killed for.

---

* Guidelines for Factual Programmes, BBC, 1989.

RIOT COVERAGE

Camera crews would soon be in danger if the public generally thought that the pictures they took were routinely passed to the authorities. (Courtesy of BBC Central Stills.)

A Journalist has no more Legal Rights than any other Citizen

Your rights

Although an image persists of camera crews and journalists armed with special powers regularly cocking a snook at authority in the pursuit of news-gathering duties, a close examination of the media's legal rights would prove their status to be no higher than that of the ordinary citizen. In reality, without the guarantees as provided by the United States Freedom of Information Act or the First Amendment to the Constitution (and in the absence so far of a pan-European Community equivalent), camera crews and journalists in Britain operate largely on the basis of custom and practice: in other words, what is accepted is what is already accepted, and any improvements are hard won in a series of very small steps.

'Public relations'

Strictly speaking, a 'journalist' in Britain has no more rights within the law than any other citizen, and negotiations over the rules governing access to places where newsworthy incidents take place are sometimes difficult and prolonged. As Britain does not have a national police force, individual area authorities have their own procedures and guidelines which form the basis of the relationship with the media, although the Association of Chief Police Officers (representing the country's Chief Constables) does seek to establish a national policy on certain issues, such as the reporting of kidnapping incidents.

In many areas Press or Public Relations departments (often staffed by civilians) are set up by the police to assist journalists in the reporting of crime, and designated Press Liaison Officers appear at the scene of major events to give what help they can, even though access to individual policemen or women directly involved may not always be encouraged. Similar arrangements are likely to be made by fire brigades and other emergency services.

Obstruction and trespass

As a camera-operator you should be aware that every time you stop to raise your camera in a public place (on the pavement, for example) you are technically causing an obstruction and the police are within their power to move you on. (Chances are you will be tolerated unless you set up a tripod.) Procedures for getting permission do exist: check with the local force.

Crews descending on scenes of public interest are likely to find themselves corralled behind crash barriers a decent distance from the action and liable to expulsion from the area if they persistently stray outside, and if the public is refused entry to a cordoned-off area 'for their own safety', being a member of a camera crew from a reputable news organization is no guarantee of exemption. The dividing line between public and private property also means that, in effect, anyone crossing it is guilty of trespass – a useful way of keeping the media at bay.

IN THE PUBLIC INTEREST: THE POLICE AND THE MEDIA*

SOME DO'S AND DON'TS

DO try to understand the needs of each other – TRUST IS A TWO-WAY PROCESS and can only be built up through working together and negotiation.

DON'T make unrealistic requests.

POLICE OFFICERS should not seize cameras, film or video at the scene – in almost every case there is no legal right to do this.

MEDIA should not expect instant access to a site – there may have been a criminal act to deal with, or it may be that the site is still dangerous and the police have an overriding duty to safeguard everybody's lives.

POLICE may clear for good operational reasons, but not just because they would rather the media was not present. Do explain why it was necessary – the media may grumble but they will understand.

On rare occasions POLICE may request CO-OPERATION from the media in delaying the release of information – but again, only for sound operational reasons, which should be clear and unambiguous; always seek the services of a senior press officer in making the arrangements.

As a member of the media you should do nothing which puts you or others at risk.

WHAT TO ALLOW AND WHAT NOT TO ALLOW

Victims and their families have the right to expect sympathetic and tasteful treatment by the media, but it is not the role of the police to set those standards or to act as censor. It is the editor who must make the decisions and it is he or she who must answer to public opinion. That does not prevent a police officer requesting the media to respect other people's privacy or requesting sensitive and compassionate behaviour.

---

* From the leaflet accompanying 'In the Public Interest', a Metropolitan Police video examining the views of police, journalists, broadcasters and editors (Extract reproduced by permission of the Directorate of Public Affairs, Metropolitan Police Service, New Scotland Yard, London).

Sensitivity and Over-sensitivity

Ethics

That TV has become the prime source of news for the majority of the British public is now an accepted fact, so it is proper to find the role of the medium in society put increasingly under the microscope. The activities of journalists and camera crews have come under particularly close scrutiny, the outcome including the establishment of an array of Codes of Conduct and the setting up of bodies such as a Broadcasting Standards Council armed with limited powers to admonish offenders.

A matter of taste

What TV viewers might find distasteful is often related directly to the time of day the programme they are watching is being transmitted: the British broadcasters' 'watershed', separating the time at which children might be among the audience from the time when they are considered not to be, is put at 9 p.m. and content adjusted accordingly. Editors of factual TV programmes are therefore bidden to bear this in mind, which means that, in theory, late evening news bulletins are freer to show particular scenes which afternoon ones are not. (There is also an increasing body of opinion which would prefer not to see anything resembling 'bad' news at any time.)

Covering 'disasters'

This problem has become more acute since the introduction of advanced technology allowed pictures from the scene of national or man-made disasters to get on air more quickly and – more importantly – live, often with little or no time for evaluation. Viewers notice this: a survey on behalf of the Broadcasting Standards Council indicated 'The picturing of the bereaved in an emotional state, the interviewing of bereaved relatives and of victims, and the showing of dead bodies, were particularly distressing'.* While your aim should be to convey the horror of a disaster, there is no merit in broadcasting lingering close-ups of recognizable bodies, bits of bodies or pools of blood, when long shots would be less distasteful and just as effective.

Over-sensitivity

There is another school of thought, to which the authors belong, which is concerned about over-sensitivity and the sanitization of news to the extent of distortion, for in the climate of opinion existing in the early nineties it is possible to imagine the disturbing pictures of suffering Romanian orphans and starving Ethiopians never reaching the screen. That they did, to create the great public response which followed, is in itself justification of the editorial decision to show them.

---

* *Survivors and the Media*, by Anne Shearer (Broadcasting Standards Monograph, 1991).

ETHICAL GUIDELINES

Death and Disaster coverage. In all circumstances you should operate in as tactful and considerate a manner as possible: most of the time common sense will dictate. It will not stop you getting the story.

Avoid

- lingering close-ups of blood
- people obviously in pain
- people dying
- intruding on bereaved relatives
- close-ups of recognizable bodies
- bits of bodies

Questions for the Future

Conclusion

The broadened range of factual TV programme services on offer from CNN, Sky News, the BBC World Service and others at the time of writing represents only a mouth-watering taste of the future. The certainty of more, slimmer, freer-wheeling, less hidebound TV journalism, supported by technological advances as yet barely thought of and changes in outdated working practices, is a fascinating and welcome one.

And yet . . . deliberately or unconsciously, we have throughout this book emphasized the importance we place on reaching and maintaining the highest possible standards of technical excellence.

To some readers impatient for their chance to embark on a career in the exciting medium of TV, this approach might seem quaint or perhaps even old-fashioned. The same applies to employers desperate for a formula to defeat the increased competition and spiralling costs at a time of economic recession.

We cannot and would not wish to stand in the way of real progress and the introduction of sensible financial controls over the enormous, often profligate, expenditure associated with much news and current affairs broadcasting. At the same time, it would not be right to ignore some of the more obvious dangers in what could be interpreted as a rush towards economies for their own sake.

Single-crewing disadvantages

As they take the place of two or three person crews, single-operators will increasingly find themselves in places where they come under intense pressure not to shoot contentious raw material in the first place. With the recordist goes the loss of the camera operator's 'second pair of eyes'. In dangerous situations, who is to provide the moral and physical support for the cameraman while he or she is glued to the viewfinder?

Multi-skilling

The deregulation of broadcasting in Britain and in many other countries has encouraged the creation of smaller, independent 'publishing houses' providing material for those transmitting the programmes. For people who work in these organizations, the opportunity to broaden their experience into complementary fields of activity – genuine 'multi-skilling' – has never been greater, and is to be welcomed enthusiastically. There remains, however, a nagging concern that despite the fact not every camera-operator will be able to write well, nor every writer operate a camera effectively, the economic pressure will be on them to try to do so, and the excellence of British broadcasting, based for so long on hard-earned specialist craft knowledge, could be slowly but irreparably eroded.

We would prefer to be optimistic and say the desire of the programme-makers to produce well-constructed material will, after all, be the overriding considera-tion, and those with the potential to learn an adjacent skill will be provided with the proper training to achieve it. But for many the temptation to start accepting only slightly lower standards in exchange for the benefits of greater flexibility and economy is bound to be extremely hard to ignore.

The great danger in all of this is that second best, once regarded as the norm, becomes very hard to displace.

Further Reading

Don't Shoot the Yanqui, by Erik Durschmied (Grafton, 1990)

Electronic News Gathering, by Robert B. Musburger (Focal Press, 1991)

From the House of War, by John Simpson (Arrow Books, 1991)

Guidelines for Factual Programmes (BBC, 1989)

News! News! News! (BBC Television Training Manual, 1991)

Single Camera Stereo Sound, by John Ratcliff and Neil Papworth (Focal Press, 1992)

Survivors and the Media, by Anne Shearer (Broadcasting Standards Monograph, 1991)

ENG Equipment Suppliers

New and used equipment
DPL Video Services, Unit 6, Wembley Park Business Centre, North End Road, Wembley, Middlesex HA9 0AG (Tel.: 081 900 1866)

Hire specialists
Optex, 22–26 Victoria Road, New Barnet, Herts EN4 9PF (Tel.: 081 441 2199)

Microwave links
Advent Communications Ltd, Alma Road, Chesham, Bucks HP5 3HE (Tel.: 0494 774 400)

Continental Microwave Ltd, 1 Crawley Green Road, Luton LU1 3LB (Tel.: 0582 424 233)

Cameras
Ampex G.B. Ltd, Acre Road, Reading, Berks SL3 9ES (Tel.: 0734 875 200)

Ikegami Electronics, Kestrel Court, Pound Road, Chertsey, Surrey KT16 8ER (Tel.: 0932 568 966)

Panasonic Broadcast Europe, 107–109 Whitby Road, Slough, Bucks SL1 3DR (Tel.: 0753 692 442)

Sony Broadcast and Communications, Jays Close, Viables, Basingstoke, Hants RG22 4SB (Tel.: 0256 55 011)

Thomson Broadcast, 18 Horton Road, Datchet, Berks SL3 9ES (Tel.: 0753 581 196)

Tripods
Sachtler (Sole Agent: Optex, as above)

Vinten Broadcast Ltd, Western Way, Bury St. Edmunds, Suffolk IP33 3TB (Tel.: 0284 750 560)

Audio mixers
SQN Sound Mixers, Unit KA, Balthane Industrial Estate, Ballasalla, Isle of Man (Tel.: 0624 824 545)

Batteries
PAG Ltd, 565 Kingston Road, London SW20 8SA (Tel.: 081 543 3131)

Lights
Arri GB Ltd, 1–3 Airlinks, Spitfire Way, Heston TW5 9NR (Tel.: 081 561 1312)

Sachtler (Sole Agent: Optex, as above)

Helicopters
Aces High Ltd, Building C1, West Wing, Fairoaks Airport, Chobham, Surrey GU24 8HU (Tel.: 0276 856 384)

Aeromega Helicopters, Hangar One, Stapleford Aerodrome, Stapleford Tawney, Essex RM4 1RL (Tel.: 081 500 3030)

Airborne TV Ltd, 8 St. Laurence Close, Orpington, Kent BR5 3LX (Tel.: 0689 897 119)

Alan Mann Helicopters Ltd, Fairoaks Airport, Chobham, Woking, Surrey GU24 8HU (Tel. 0276 857 471)

Lenses
Canon UK Ltd, Canon House, Manor Road, Wallington, Surrey SM6 0AJ (Tel.: 081 773 3173)

Fuji, c/o Pyser-SGI Ltd, Broadcast and CCTV Division, Fircroft Way, Edenbridge, Kent TN8 6HN (Tel.: 0732 864 111)

Telephone broadcast equipment
Gavan E. Kelly Ltd, 245 Kingston Road, Kingston-on-Thames, Surrey KT2 5JH (Tel.: 081 549 3863)

Videotapes
Ampex G.B. Ltd, Acre Road, Reading, Berks SL3 9ES (Tel.: 0734 875 200)

Feltec Electronics, Unit 3U St. Albans Enterprise Centre, Long Spring, Porters Wood, St. Albans, Herts AL3 6EN (Tel.: 0727 834 888)

3M UK PLC, 3M House, P.O. Box 1, Bracknell, Berks RG12 1JU (Tel.: 0344 426 726)

Sony Broadcast and Communications, Jays Close, Viables, Basingstoke, Hants RG22 4SB (Tel.: 0256 55 011)

Microphones
Bayer Dynamic GB Ltd, Unit 14, Cliffe Industrial Estate, Lewes, East Sussex BN8 6JL (Tel.: 0273 479 411)

Sennheiser UK Ltd, 12 Davies Way, Knaves Beech Business Centre, Loudwater, High Wycombe, Bucks HP10 9QY (Tel.: 0628 850 811)

Sony Broadcast and Communications, Jays Close, Viables, Basingstoke, Hants RG22 4SB (Tel.: 0256 55 011)

Radio microphones
Audio Engineering Ltd, Fitzroy House, Abbot Street, London E8 3LP (Tel.: 071 254 5475)

Useful Contacts in UK Broadcasting

Career and Training advice
BBC Corporate Recruitment, Portland Place, London W1 (Tel.: 071 580 4468)

British Kinematograph, Sound and Television Society, 547 Victoria House, Vernon Place, London WC1B 4DJ (Tel.: 071 242 8400)

Broadcasting and Entertainment Trades and Cinematographic Theatre Union (BECTU), 111 Wardour Street, London W1V 4AY (Tel.: 071 437 8506)

Skillset, 60 Charlotte Street, London W1 (Tel.: 071 927 8568)

Centre for Journalism Studies, University College of Wales, Cardiff CF1 3AS (Tel.: 0222 984 786)

City University, Graduate Centre for Journalism, St. John Street, London EC1V 0HB (Tel.: 071 253 4399)

Darlington College of Technology, Cleveland Avenue, Darlington DL3 7BB (Tel.: 0325 467 651)

Falmouth School of Art and Design, Wood Lane, Falmouth, Cornwall TR11 4RA (Tel.: 0326 211 077)

Highbury College of Technology, Dovercourt Road, Cosham, Portsmouth PO6 2SA (Tel.: 0705 383 181)

National Council for the Training of Broadcast Journalists, 188 Lichfield Court, Sheen Road, Richmond TW9 1BB (Tel.: 081 940 0694)

National Film and Television School, Beaconsfield Studios, Station Road, Beaconsfield, Bucks (Tel.: 0494 677 903)

Producers Alliance for Cinema and Television (PACT), Gordon House, Green-coat Place, London SW1P 1PH (Tel.: 071 233 6000)

Royal Television Society Training Department, Holborn Hall, 100 Gray's Inn Road, London, WC1X 8AL (Tel.: 071 430 1000)

University of Central Lancashire, Preston, Lancs PR1 2TQ (Tel.: 0772 22 141)

University of the West of England at Bristol, Clanage Road, Bower Ashton, Bristol BS3 2JU (Tel.: 0272 660 222)

University of Westminster, 18 Riding House Street, London W1 (Tel.: 071 911 5000)

Television organizations
Anglia Television, Anglia House, Norwich, Norfolk NR1 3JG (Tel.: 0603 615 151)

BBC Midlands, Broadcasting Centre, Pebble Mill Road, Birmingham B5 7SA (Tel.: 021 418 8888)

BBC North, New Broadcasting House, Oxford Road, Manchester M60 1SJ (Tel.: 061 200 2020)

BBC Northern Ireland, Broadcasting House, Ormeau Avenue, Belfast BT2 8HQ (Tel.: 0232 244 400)

BBC Regional Broadcasting, White City, 201 Wood Lane, London W12 7TS (Tel.: 081 752 5252)

BBC Scotland, Broadcasting House, Queen Margaret Drive, Glasgow G12 8DG (Tel.: 041 330 2345)

BBC South, Broadcasting House, Whiteladies Road, Bristol BS8 2LR (Tel.: 0272 732 211)

BBC Wales, Broadcasting House, Llandaff, Cardiff CF5 2YQ (Tel.: 0222 572 888)

Border Television, Television Centre, Carlisle, Cumbria CA1 3NT (Tel.: 0228 25 101)

British Sky Broadcasting, 6 Centaurs Business Park, Grant Way, Syon Lane, Isleworth, Middlesex TW7 5QL (Tel.: 071 782 3000)

Carlton Television, 101 St. Martin's Lane, London WC2N 4AZ (Tel.: 071 240 4000)

Central Television, Central House, Birmingham B1 2JP (Tel.: 021 643 9898)

Channel Television, The TV Centre, La Pouquelaye, St. Helier, Jersey, CI (Tel.: 0534 68 999)

Channel 4 Television, 60 Charlotte Street, London W1P 2AX (Tel.: 071 631 4444)

CNN International, CNN House, 19 Rathbone Place, London W1P 1DF (Tel.: 071 637 6700)

GMTV, The London Television Centre, Upper Ground, London SE1 9LT (Tel.: 071 261 8020)

Grampian Television, Queen's Cross, Aberdeen AB9 2XJ (Tel.: 0224 646 464)

Granada Television, Quay Street, Manchester M60 9EA (Tel.: 061 832 7211)

HTV, Culverhouse Cross, Cardiff CF5 6XJ (Tel.: 0222 590 590)

Independent Television News, 200 Gray's Inn Road, London WC1 8XZ (Tel.: 071 833 3000)

London Weekend Television, Upper Ground, London SE1 9LT (Tel.: 071 620 1620)

Meridian Broadcasting, TV Centre, Northam Road, Southampton SO9 5HZ (Tel.: 0703 222 555)

Reuters Television (formally Visnews), Cumberland Avenue, London NW10 7EH (Tel.: 081 965 7733)

Scottish Television, Cowcaddens, Glasgow G2 3PR (Tel.: 041 332 9999)

Tyne Tees Television, City Road, Newcastle on Tyne NE1 2AL (Tel.: 091 261 0181)

Ulster Television, Havelock House, Ormeau Road, Belfast BT7 1EB (Tel.: 0232 328 122)

Westcountry Television, Millbay Docks, Plymouth PL1 3EW (Tel.: 0752 253 322)

Worldwide Television News, The Interchange, 21 Oval Road, London NW1 (Tel.: 071 413 8300)

Yorkshire Television, The Television Centre, Leeds LS3 1JS (Tel.: 0532 438 283)

Useful publications include:
Weeklies
Broadcast, 7 Swallow Place, London W1R 7AA

UK Press Gazette, Maclean Hunter House, Chalk Lane, Cockfosters Road, Barnet, Herts EN4 0BU

Monthlies
International Broadcasting, 7 Swallow Place, London W1R 7AA

Televisual, St. Giles House, 50 Poland Street, London W1V 4AX

World Broadcast News, 38th Floor, 888 7th Avenue, New York, NY 10106

Glossary

Additive primary colours   Red, green and blue. The basis of colour TV. Mixing these three colours in the correct proportions will produce white light.

AGC   Automatic gain control. An amplifier used in audio and video circuits to correct input signal variations and produce a satisfactory output.

Ambient sound   Noise, reverberation or atmospheric sounds in the background to a principal audio source.

Amps   Amperes. The unit of measurement for an electric current.

Analogue   An electronic signal which depends on varying voltage levels. For example those produced from a microphone or the camera's CCD.

Audio frequency   The human ear's frequency response, which ranges from about 15Hz to 20kHz.

Audio isolating transformer   A small device which isolates the d.c. component of a sound circuit, allowing the analogue signal to pass with no significant loss of power but allowing voltage and impedence matching.

AVC   Automatic volume control (see Limiter and Compressor).

Back focus   The distance separating the vortex of the back surface of a lens and the CCD when the lens is set on infinity.

Bandwidth   The range of frequencies occupied by a video or audio signal. The higher the frequency range, the wider the required bandwidth.

Betacam   12.5mm video format developed by Sony.

Betecam SP   SP – Superior Performance. Advanced basic Betacam system.

Black balance   An operation to balance the additive primary colours of red, green and blue so their blacks have no colour.

Black and burst   Colour video signal containing no picture information but the colour burst signal, sync. pulses and black level (see Colour Burst).

BNC   Twist-type video cable connector.

Capacitance   Component comprising conducting plates separated by an insulator called a dielectric.

Capstan   Video-recorder drive mechanism which moves the oxide tape at a specified speed. Its rotation usually synchronizes with the reference sync signal.

Cardioid microphone   Specialized unidirectional microphone with a heart-shaped polar pick-up response.

CCD   Charged coupled device. Solid-state light-sensitive device used in optical scanning in cameras and telecine machines. CCDs have replaced the tube in ENG cameras. They have no image lag or burn.

Character generator   Post-production device used to generate a visible time code and other digital information.

Chroma   The amount of colour information or the level of colour in a TV picture. If it is too low, the picture will look pale and washed out. With high-level colours the picture will look saturated.

Chroma key   Electronic process for combining two or more video images into a composite picture without one 'bleeding' into another. Recent years have seen the development of highly sophisticated matting processes.

Coincident pairs   Arrangement for stereophony in which two microphones are placed with their diaphragms in different directions but so close together that the path length between the audio source and both microphones is equal and in phase. They are often housed in the same capsule.

Colour balance The adjustment of colour to a given reference so that all cameras, tape machines and monitors see the same colour value of a given object.

Colour bars Electronically generated standard reference signal. They include the three additive primary colours (red, green and blue) and the three subtractive primary colours (yellow, magenta and cyan). A minimum of 30 seconds of colour bars should be recorded on the beginning of each tape.

Colour burst (or Colour sub-carrier) Colour reference signal inserted into every video line. Determines how the colour information is to be interpreted.

Colour signal Chrominance portion of the video signal. Represented by C.

Comet tail Trail from a moving light source. Caused by image retention in some tubes and circuitry when shooting at night.

Companding Opposite of Compression (q.v.).

Complementary colours Cyan, magenta and yellow. Result of mixing parts of the primary colours.

Component video Signal with the colour information in three separate signals – red, green and blue.

Composite video Signal consisting of video (luminance and colour sub-carrier), sync (horizontal and vertical) and the colour burst signal. The information is encoded into a single signal.

Compressor Circuit designed to reduce automatically the dynamic range of the audio signal.

Compression Video circuit designed to data compress digital video signals.

Condenser microphone Transducer which converts sound waves by conductive principles. Needs a built-in power source or phantom power from the camera or mixer.

Control track Electronic sprocket hole system recorded on to videotape to maintain constant speed.

DA Distribution amplifier. Provides multiple video and/or audio outlets for news conferences, etc.

Decibel (db) Acoustic measurement following logarithmic law (as does the human ear) in relating sound intensity to sensation. One-tenth of a bel. The decibel is considered to be the minimun change in level the ear can perceive.

Degausser Unit used to erase magnetic tapes in bulk.

Dichroic In ENG, usually the blue glass filter which shifts a tungsten colour balance source from 3200 degrees Kelvin to the daylight 5600K.

Digital Electronic state composed of binary 1 and 0.

Digital audio tape Recording system superior to standard analogue.

Digital formats D1 – 19mm component; D2 – 19mm composite; D3 – 12.5mm Panasonic composite. (Potential: D4 – Ampex component; D5 – 12.5mm Panasonic; D6 – 12.5mm data-compressed Beta derivative; D7 – 19mm data-compressed component; D8 – 8mm Sony, as yet unspecified.)

Digital video Video signal made up of assigned numbers rather than analogue voltage. Provides high-quality videotape recording.

Dioptre Simple supplementary lens which can be fitted to a standard lens to increase wide-angle capability.

Disc recorder See Video Disc.

Dolby Noise reduction system invented by Ray Dolby.

Dynamic contrast control Circuit allowing the video camera to accept a picture of wide luminance and dynamic range.

184

Dynamic microphone   Omnidirectional microphone.

E to E   Electronic to electronic. Refers to the input signal fed to the recorder and monitored direct on the output, not the videotape.
Electrostatic microphone   See Condenser Microphone.
Expander   Amplifier which increases in gain as the amplitude increases. Opposite of compression.

F stop   Scale used to calibrate the speed of lenses.
Field   One-half of a complete television picture. 312.5 lines of the 625-line PAL system.
Fluorescent light   System in which ionized gases in the tube emit a mix of colour temperatures. Modern video cameras, when properly balanced to that source, cope superbly.
FM   Frequency modulation. Method of modulating the carrier by varying its frequency, as distinct from amplitude modulation. Channels 3 and 4 are the usual ENG FM audio recording channels.
Foot-candle   Amount of light falling on an area one foot square and one foot from the candle.
Frame synchronizer   Unit accepting non-synchronized video, stores it for a full frame and feeds the signals, properly timed, into the rest of the system.

Gamma   Measure of total contrast in a scene. In a multi-camera set-up, given that the gammas are the same, pictures should match perfectly.
Gen lock   Method of synchronizing or electronically locking several video sources.
Giga   1 000 000 000 or 10^9. Symbol G.
Gray scale   Test pattern in steps from white to black used by engineers to fine tune cameras.

HAD   Sony's Hole Accumulated Diode. Type of semiconductor enabling CCDs to reduce stationary noise.
HDTV   High definition television.
Helical scan   Recording system which wraps the tape round the video scanner in a helix pattern.
Hi8   Sony 8mm high-performance camcorder.
HMI   Metal halide discharge lamps operating at 5600K (daylight).

Impedance   Measured in ohms, combines resistance, inductance and capacitance to reduce signals in an a.c. circuit.
Inductance   Created when a circuit with stronger magnetic field induces some of its signals into a circuit with a weaker magnetic field.
ISO   Isolated camera. Used in multi-camera systems to provide separate, unedited output, bypassing the video mixer.
IT   Interline transfer. Type of CCD imager.

Kelvin   Measurement of the relative colour of light.
Kilo   1000 or 10^3. Symbol k.

Lag-smear   See Comet Tail.
Limiter   Device through which programmes can be processed without gain or alteration of the signal until a critical value is reached, usually at a point just before overload distortion could occur.

LNG Longitudinal recording. Where the sound signal is recorded along the tape path on the audio track.

LTC Longitudinal time code. Control track recorded on a dedicated channel or audio track.

Luminance (Y) Monochrome component of the colour video signal.

Lux Unit used to measure light levels. There are 10.76 lux to a foot-candle.

M1 12.5mm upgraded component VHS video format.

M11 Improved M1.

Macro Optical device built into most zoom lenses to facilitate high-quality close-up shooting.

Matte box Lens protection device.

Mega 1 000 000 or 10^6. Symbol M.

Milli 1/1000 or 10^{-3}. Symbol m.

Micro 1/1 000 000 or 10^{-6}. Symbol μ.

MOD Minimum optical distance. The closest point to the front element of a lens at which an object will be in focus.

Multiplex Combination of multiple signals into a single feed for transmission purposes.

Nano 1/1 000 000 000 or 10^{-9}. Symbol n.

Neutral density filter A filter which does not correct the colour signal but attenuates the luminance level.

NICAM Near instantaneously companded audio multiplex. Digital transmission system bringing CD stereo quality sound to the domestic television receiver.

NTSC National Television Standards Committee founded in the USA in 1940. Name given to the American colour TV system.

OB Multi-camera live outside broadcast.

Off-line editing Viewing and decision-making process of material using non-broadcast-quality equipment. Usually includes time code to facilitate transfer to on-line editing (q.v.).

Omnidirectional microphone Microphone with 360-degree polar response. Responds equally to audio from all sources.

On-line editing Final assembly of broadcast-quality master tape.

Oxides Coating on tape which responds to electromagnetic signals.

PAL Phase alternate line. European broadcast transmission standard.

Pan pot. Panoramic potentiometer. Pair of ganged potentiometers with which a sound source can be divided differentially between the stereo channels to a place in a desired location in the sound image.

Peak white Whitest portion of the video signal.

Pedestal or black level Blackest point in the video picture.

Phantom power Method of sending d.c. power to a condenser microphone. Most ENG cameras have a 48V supply.

Pixel Picture element. The smallest element of a scan line sampled on a CCD, which may have as many as 500 000.

Primary colours. See Additive Primary Colours.

Proc Amp Process amplifier. System to strip distorted syncs from a video playback signal and replaces them with clean syncs.

Quad Two-inch black and white video broadcast format originated by Ampex.

Raster Illuminated video signal on the face of the picture tube: the scanning pattern without the picture.

Resistance Measurement in ohms indicating the constraints to electricity flow.

RF Radio frequency.

SECAM Séquentiel Couleur à Mémoire. The French 625-line 50Hz transmission standard.

Signal-to-noise ratio Relationship of the strength of the audio or video signals to the noise which can be seen or heard.

SIS Sound in syncs. Combination of the sound and video signals. Audio is sent in a pulse code modulated (digital) form during the line synchronizing period of the video waveform.

SMPTE US-based Society of Motion Picture and Television Engineers.

Standards converter Unit designed to convert one television standard to another; for example, from NTSC 525 lines to PAL 625.

Sub-carrier See Colour Burst.

Subtractive primary colours Yellow, magenta, cyan.

S-VHS Super or separate VHS amateur/professional video standard.

Sync generator Unit providing sync signals, drive, blanking and sync pulses to stabilize and lock video systems.

TBC Time-base corrector. Device for correcting time-base errors in videotape playback.

Time code Numbering system by which audio and video signals are identified for editing and reference. Based on 24-hour clock time.

Transducer Device converting one form of energy to another; for example, camera transduces light to electronic video signals.

U bits Section of the time code in which to record supplementary information.

U matic 19mm format. The first ENG.

Unidirectional Microphone with pick-up characteristic from a single direction; for example a gun mike.

Up link Transmission path from ground station to satellite.

VCR Video cassette recorder.

Vectorscope Cathode ray tube unit designed to give a graphic display of the colour proportion of the video signal.

Vertical interval time code Time code converted to video information and recorded in the interval during the scanning of the cathode ray tube.

Vertical smear Smear caused by pinpoints of specular or bright light against a dark background, resulting in overload of the CCD.

VHS 12.5mm video home systems format.

Video disc Digital device used mainly for storing still frames and graphics. Complementary home entertainment system to VCR.

Volts Pressure of electricity.

VTR Video tape recorder.

Vu meter Volume unit meter. Displays average audio peak power levels.

Waveform monitor Cathode ray tube unit designed to give a graphic display of the black and white part of the video signal.

White balance Electronic matching of the camera circuits to the colour temperature of the light source.

187

XLR plug/socket Professional three-pin audio connector.

Y Denotes luminance element in the colour video signal.

Zebra pattern Pattern which appears on a camera viewfinder to help in obtaining correct exposure.

media MANUAL

Introduction to ENG

£12-95